A DETAILED ANALYSIS
of the
CONSTITUTION

A DETAILED ANALYSIS
of the
CONSTITUTION

Edward F. Cooke

Sixth Edition

LITTLEFIELD ADAMS QUALITY PAPERBACKS

LITTLEFIELD ADAMS QUALITY PAPERBACKS

a division of Rowman & Littlefield Publishers, Inc.
4720 Boston Way, Lanham, Maryland 20706

Published in the United States of America

British Cataloging in Publication Information Available

Library of Congress Cataloging-in-Publication Data

Cooke, Edward Francis
A detailed analysis of the Constitution / by Edward F. Cooke.—
6th ed.
p. cm.
Includes index.
1. United States—Constitutional law. I. Title.
KF4550.Z9C676 1995   342.73' 023—dc20   94-23358 CIP
                           [347.30223]

ISBN 0–8226–3037–0 (pbk: alk. paper)
Printed in the United States of America

The paper used in this publication meets the minimum requirements of American National Standard for Information Sciences— Permanence of Paper for Printed Library Materials, ANSI Z39.48-1984.

I dedicate this book to my wife, Dorothy M. Cooke, whose love, guidance, and support I dearly cherish.

E.F.C.

CONTENTS

INTRODUCTION

Accounts of budget crises, trade agreements, special prosecutors, potential impeachment, congressional hearings, abortion demonstrations, and other problems in our daily papers and TV newscasts provide ample evidence that the national Constitution and its interpretations have a vital impact on contemporary American society. The United States is unique among nations in that many political, economic, and social issues are discussed and resolved within the framework of our legal system. For this reason, the Constitution and its interpreters, the judges, play a significant role in American government and politics.

This book on the Constitution, though intended primarily to enrich and supplement the standard texts in history and government, also serves as a guide and reference for all citizens who are interested in the development of American institutions. The concise analysis of the meanings of the several sections of the Constitution, together with the expositions on the history and principles of constitutionalism, will, it is believed, stimulate respect for and study of the basic law of the land.

E.F.C.

A DETAILED ANALYSIS
of the
CONSTITUTION

Chapter 1

Making the United States Constitution

The history of the U.S. Constitution illustrates the faith and confidence that the framers had in themselves and in the institutions they created. The constitution drafted in Philadelphia in 1787 was more than the product of idealistic dreams. It was founded on experience coupled with great wisdom. Principles long cherished by Americans were no mere "spur of the moment" thoughts of wise men; they were, and still are, enduring fundamentals. Many of them evolved from the fact that the United States had operated within other, less formalized frameworks of government before the adoption of the Constitution. This chapter describes these experiences in union-making and illustrates how the founding fathers incorporated the good of past systems into our basic law.

The Early Beginnings

New England Confederation. As early as 1643, Americans were thinking in terms of a union. In that year the colonies of Massachusetts Bay, Plymouth, Connecticut, and New Haven formed the New England Confederation for the purpose of planning joint campaigns against the Indians. The Confederation also had authority over disputes involving boundaries, fugitive criminals, and slaves. Although the Confederation was not an outstanding success, it functioned until 1684.

Dominion of New England. The British took a hand in union-making in 1686. As a means of achieving more control and efficiency in the colonial governments, the Crown created the Dominion of New England. All the New England colonies, New York, and New Jersey were placed under the authority of one royal governor. When James II was dethroned in 1689, the Dominion quickly collapsed.

Albany Plan. The French and Indian Wars had shown both British and American leaders the necessity for unification. At the Albany Conference, called by the British in 1754, Benjamin Franklin presented a plan of union. With a few changes, the Conference adopted the so-called Albany Plan and recommended it to the colonies. Not a single colonial legislature, however, accepted the plan. Nor did the English authorities favor it. Each side believed that the Albany Plan gave too much power to the other.

First Continental Congress. A decade before the outbreak of fighting at Concord Bridge, representatives from nine colonies had met simply to voice protest against the Stamp Act. At the request of Massachusetts and Virginia, a second meeting was held in 1774. *The First Continental Congress,* as this meeting is known, had no legal authority to act for all the colonies. It was called entirely in response to the common demand of the people. This Congress passed a series of resolutions that stated the colonial position on taxation, representation, and other matters. To put teeth into its action, the Congress also adopted a boycott on English-made goods, and recommended another meeting the following year.

Second Continental Congress. The Second Continental Congress met in 1775 and was attended by delegates from all the colonies. This Congress likewise had no formal legal basis since there was no constitution or written agreement to give it the authority to act. Its power stemmed from the common consent of the people. The fact that no group opposed its actions, in effect, constituted approval. Conditions had changed since the First Continental Congress. Fighting had begun. Men who had been chosen to express the colonial point of view and, perhaps, to bargain with the British authorities, now were faced with the problem of waging a war. In addition, individual colonies were asking for advice on their status within the empire. Hesitantly, the Congress advised them to establish their own governments.

Starting without funds, without equipment, and without personnel, an army was created, manned, and financed by the Congress. Help from foreign countries was obtained. By any and all means, the Congress held the separate, independent states together. Far from the temporary body it set out to be, this Congress lasted until 1781.

The Articles of Confederation, a compact of the states, replaced the Congress as the governing body of the new nation in 1781. Shining like a beacon light in the brief history of the Second Continental Congress was America's answer to arbitrary, autocratic government— the Declaration of Independence.

The Declaration of Independence

Clashes between the American and British forces had been taking place for over a year before Richard Henry Lee of Virginia introduced a resolution in Congress on June 7, 1776. His resolution provided for a proclamation of independence, an authorization to enter into foreign alliances and plan for some form of a union.

A few states were hesitant to take such a drastic step so soon; still other states, particularly in New England, were openly and eagerly seeking independence. The members of the Continental Congress discussed the problem at length. Thomas Jefferson took the major responsibility for formulating the Declaration, though John Adams and Benjamin Franklin contributed suggestions. Finally, crucial votes were taken on July 1 and July 2 and the Declaration was formally adopted on July 4, 1776.

Philosophy of the Declaration. The Declaration of Independence is one of our most treasured documents, not because it is old, but because it still has meaning for us today. Naturally it was aimed at King George III and charged him with permitting a long list of abuses. These were important to the Americans of the Revolution. Equally important to them and perhaps more important to us today is the philosophy of government which is so nobly expressed in the opening paragraphs:

> WE HOLD THESE TRUTHS TO BE SELF-EVIDENT, THAT ALL MEN ARE CREATED EQUAL, THAT THEY ARE ENDOWED BY THEIR CREATOR WITH CERTAIN UNALIENABLE RIGHTS, THAT AMONG THESE ARE LIFE, LIBERTY AND THE PURSUIT OF HAPPINESS, THAT TO SECURE THESE RIGHTS, GOVERNMENTS ARE INSTITUTED AMONG MEN, DERIVING THEIR JUST POWERS FROM THE CONSENT OF THE GOVERNED.

This is the philosophy of natural rights, of limited government, of popular control, of the social contract, and of justification for rebellion. Jefferson does not say that all men are physically equal, but that they are equal under the law. There shall not be one law for the rich and another for the poor. Jefferson is saying that man has certain natural rights which belong to him because he is a man, a human being. These rights cannot be taken away, because man has created a limited government for the very purpose of protecting rights. This philosophy had a real meaning to the early Americans; they later constructed a government based upon such ideas. This philosophy has meaning for us today because we live under such a government.

The Articles of Confederation

As the fighting wore on, a number of men saw the need for a more permanent foundation for the new states. The Continental Congress existed under no constitution or law; it had only the war crisis to draw and hold the people together. Therefore a committee was appointed to draft a constitution. The Congress approved this constitution in 1778 and submitted it to the states for their approval because the new instrument of government could not become effective until all states had ratified it.

Most of the states ratified it very quickly, but a few states, particularly Maryland, were reluctant to do so until the conflicting claims of the states to western lands had been settled. Given adequate assurances that the land would be turned over to all the states (i.e., the United States), Maryland finally approved it in 1781, and the new government came into being.

Government Under the Articles. It is difficult to say what type of government existed under the Articles of Confederation, as the new constitution was called. Essentially it was a confederation—a loosely allied league of separate states. The great mass of powers was retained by the states, and only those few powers that might affect all the states—declaring war, making treaties, sending and receiving ambassadors, and coining money—were specifically given to the Confederate government. The Confederate Congress was the main branch of government. In fact, there were neither executive nor judicial branches. Each state sent, and paid expenses for, two to seven delegates to the Congress. However, each state only had one vote in the single-house legislature.

The period of the Confederation (1781–1789) was a most trying one for the infant nation. The Revolutionary War had bankrupt not only the Confederation, but also most of the states. Inflation had set in, and numerous citizens were deeply in debt. The Congress was practically powerless to deal with these mounting troubles. For one thing, it felt the loss of the outstanding leaders of the war years who had since retired from public office. Second, the Congress was stymied by certain weaknesses or defects in the framework of the government itself.

Defects in the Articles. (1) The Confederate government lacked the power to act directly upon individuals. It could act upon the people only through the agency of the states. A person was a citizen of a state and not of the United States. For example, although Congress had the power to raise and maintain an army, it had to request the states to provide the men—and, often as not, the states did not send men.

(2) The Confederate government lacked the power to operate effectively and efficiently. Even in those fields where Congress could

legislate, the more important measures, like borrowing money, required the concurrence of nine states. Sometimes, only a few states were in attendance. Furthermore, there was no real executive, but merely a committee of Congress charged with the duty of carrying out the legislature's orders. A court system was also lacking, although a special court could be set up to settle disputes between states. Here again, the system broke down since there was no method for enforcing the decision of such a tribunal.

(3) The Confederate government lacked the power to raise adequate revenue. Congress could only requisition funds from the states. The latter, barely able to maintain their own governmental operations, paid little attention to these money requests from Congress.

(4) The Confederate government lacked the power to regulate and control interstate and foreign commerce. The financially embarrassed states sought to relieve their own citizens' tax burdens by imposing all kinds of taxes on goods coming in from other states or from foreign countries. Home industries and businesses were favored, but only at the price of ruinous taxation of commerce from other states. As high as Connecticut taxed Massachusetts fish, Massachusetts would tax hats from Connecticut. Even high tariffs exacted on foreign-made products did not prevent foreign competitors from dumping their goods on an already inflationary market, further disrupting the American economy. In their zeal for revenue, the states ignored or evaded Congress's control over foreign commerce. Realizing the Confederation's impotency in enforcing treaty obligations, foreign nations began to dicker directly with the states for trading concessions.

Such a weak, chaotic system could not survive long without either a total disruption of the confederacy or a strong counter movement toward a more efficient, workable arrangement. Fortunately, the latter course prevailed, primarily as a result of the breakdown in commerce.

Preliminaries to the Constitution. In 1785 officials from the states of Maryland and Virginia met to discuss problems concerning navigation on the Potomac River. The results were so favorable that the Virginia legislature, under the leadership of James Madison, passed a resolution inviting all states to a convention at Annapolis, Maryland, the following year for the purpose of discussing commercial problems common to all states.

At the appointed time in September of 1786, delegates from only five states showed up. Far from being discouraged, this small group addressed a resolution to the Confederate Congress asking it to call another convention in 1787. Recent research indicates that a number of prominent men may have known that the Annapolis Convention was merely a preliminary to a larger and bolder assembly and did not bother to attend.

Upon receipt of the Annapolis resolution, the Congress passed its own resolution authorizing a conference to be held in Philadelphia in May, 1787, "for the sole and express purpose of revising the Articles of Confederation."

The Constitutional Convention

All the states, except Rhode Island, responded to the call by sending their foremost citizens to the Philadelphia Convention. The great leaders of the war years—Washington, Franklin, Hamilton, Madison, and Dickinson—now combined their talents and experience to undertake the task of welding the states together.

It was quickly agreed that the meetings of the convention should be secret in order that differences might be reconciled without fear of public censure or loss of confidence. Furthermore, each state was entitled to only one vote, regardless of how many delegates it had sent.

Plans of Government. The differences among the delegates, especially between those from small and large states, were recognized very early in the proceedings. The point of view of the smaller states was summed up in the plan submitted by the delegates from New Jersey. This New Jersey plan was primarily a revision of the Articles, since a single-house legislature was to be retained with its equality of representation. Minor alterations, such as separate executive and judicial branches, were also provided. The larger, wealthier states tended to favor the Virginia plan, which contemplated such extensive revisions as creating an entirely new governmental system. Separate executive and judicial branches would share considerable governmental power with a two-house legislature. In each of these houses, representation would be based upon a proportional principle.

Compromises. The practical statesmen of the convention sought and achieved a meeting of minds by encompassing the main points of each plan in the so-called Connecticut Compromise. A bicameral legislature prevailed, but in one house, each state would have equality of representation; in the other house, representation would be based upon population. Once this thorny problem was resolved, other differences involving slaves, taxation, the chief executive, and commerce were likewise settled by compromises. No one side or group imposed its will upon others. The men meeting in Philadelphia in the spring of 1787 were there to construct a workable machinery of government satisfactory to all segments and sections of the nation. To achieve this end, they had to compromise on many points. Compromise was so much the keynote of the convention that the Constitution is sometimes referred to as a "bundle of compromises."

Nevertheless, even with this apparent harmony, a number of delegates were disturbed. Most of the delegates had been instructed, expressly or implicitly, to revise the existing Articles. These instructions from either their state governors or legislatures (since no delegation was selected directly by the people) scarcely warranted substituting one framework of government for another. There was little doubt in the minds of the framers that they had done this very thing. Hamilton's and Madison's arguments, however, persuaded the hesitant delegates by pointing out the pressing need for an extensive overhaul of the existing government in order to preserve the Union. Mere revision would not suffice. Furthermore, the action of the Convention was not final. The new Constitution, in order to be effective, needed the assent of at least three-fourths of the states. Most of the doubters having been won over by these arguments, a majority of the delegates, including at least one from each of the twelve states (since Rhode Island had not participated) approved the document by affixing their signatures to its last page.

Ratification of the Constitution

Washington, as president of the Philadelphia Convention, forwarded the proposed Constitution to the Confederate Congress with the recommendation that it be submitted to the individual states for their ratification. The framers of the Constitution made two additional requests of the Congress:

(1) That in each state the new Constitution be submitted to conventions especially chosen for that purpose.

(2) That the new government become effective after nine states had ratified it.

These two stipulations were very important because the framers were trying to anticipate criticism before it could arise. The first condition would give the new Constitution a firmer foundation with respect to popular consent. Objections had been raised to the old Articles of Confederation because it had not been submitted for popular approval. The second condition attempted to avoid delay in setting up the new government. Under the Articles, the consent of all states was required for amendments. This new method of ratification was not only a tacit admission that a new fundamental law was being established, but it also destroyed the legal continuity between the Articles and the Constitution.

Ratification Campaigns. The Congress agreed to both suggestion and, without comment, referred the new Constitution to the states on September 28, 1787. Up and down the land, tremendous debates broke out concerning the merits and defects of the proposed Constitution. Arguments that had gone on for weeks during the convention were rehashed and new ones were introduced. Numerous objections were raised: some thought the new government would be too powerful, others thought it too weak. Still others feared the taxing power of Congress, while debtor groups were worried about their paper money. It became common to identify those who favored the Constitution by the name of *Federalists* and those who opposed its adoption by the term *Anti-Federalists.* Whatever their feelings on specific sections of the Constitution, a great number of persons in many states were critical because it lacked a bill of rights. The Federalist argument that the Constitution itself was a bill of rights, since the government was limited to only those powers so delegated, did not abate this objection. Federalist leaders in several states had to promise to use their influence in the new government for the passage of amendments providing for these basic liberties.

Although the delegates from the small states were among the chief criticizers during the convention deliberations, when the time for ratification came, these smaller states were the first to approve. Delaware led off on December 7, 1787, closely followed by New Jersey, Georgia, Connecticut, and Pennsylvania. Massachusetts, Maryland, South Carolina, and New Hampshire brought the number up to nine by mid-1788. The important state of Virginia finally approved, leaving New York to offer the last crucial ratification.

The Federalist Papers. Even though the requisite number of states had ratified, and plans were being made to put the Constitution into effect, New York's approval was a necessity. Besides being a populous, wealthy state, its geographic location was such that it could disrupt any union of states in which it was not a member. A tremendous campaign was waged by both Federalists and Anti-Federalists in an attempt to sway the decision of the convention. Out of this struggle emerged one of the most systematic expositions on the Constitution that has ever been written. First appearing as a series of articles in New York newspapers under the name *Publius,* these eighty-five essays were later collected in one volume and have been labeled by American scholars as *The Federalist Papers.* Hamilton, John Jay, and Madison were the real authors of the articles which were instrumental in influencing New York's ratification.

Meanwhile steps had been taken for the election of senators, representatives, and presidential electors. New York was selected as a temporary capitol. The Confederate Congress, seeing the handwriting on the political wall, quietly died by default as an insufficient number of members showed up to transact any business. Finally, the new House of Representatives and new Senate took their seats, the presidential oath was administered to George Washington, and the new government began to function.

You will remember, only eleven states had ratified the Constitution. North Carolina and Rhode Island still remained outside the Union, but this situation did not worry the leaders of the new government. Neither state was so populous, wealthy, or strategically located as to cause difficulties. In fact, it was to their economic advantage to join, which both states did, in 1790.

Sources of the Constitution

That precious document so carefully drafted by the Philadelphia Convention, over 205 years ago, is still the basic fundamental law of the United States today. No other nation in the entire world has maintained a written constitution as long as the United States. In order to be such a stable framework of government, our Constitution must have had its roots firmly implanted in principles and practices which men everywhere had considered essential to representative government.

English Sources. We can find provisions in our Constitution that date as far back as the Magna Carta of 1215. Trial by jury, due process of law, and no taxation without representation are some of the principles which the English barons forced King John to agree to in that year. Many of the guarantees of liberty and freedom contained in our Bill of Rights (the first ten amendments) owe their origin to the English people's Petition of Rights of 1628 and Bill of Rights of 1688. Our legislatures, both national and state, owe much of their form and procedure to the English Parliament.

Philosophers. The great English philosopher John Locke is often called the "Philosopher of the Revolution," because so many of his ideas were used by the colonists in support of their grievances against the British authorities. Such principles as limited government, consent of the governed, and religious tolerance stem from Locke's writings. Joseph Harrington was another English philosopher from whom the framers borrowed such ideas as separation of powers, a written constitution, and rotation in office. The French philosopher Montesquieu wrote convincingly about limited government, separation of powers, and checks and balances. To Sir Edward Coke and Sir William Blackstone, English lawyers, the Americans owed much of their knowledge of and respect for common law. This law, based on thousands of decisions handed down by judges in specific cases, is the backbone of the American legal system.

Experience. Notwithstanding these outstanding obligations to foreign sources, the framers of our Constitution drew heavily upon our rich American experience. Americans had been forming and managing governments for a century and a half before they drafted the Constitution. The very founding of the original colonies provided them with concrete examples of constitutional principles. The Mayflower Compact, an agreement among the Puritan settlers to establish a government in the wilderness, was early evidence that governments existed by virtue of the consent of the governed. The people of Rhode Island and Connecticut had also drafted their own charters of government. The colonies of Virginia and Massachusetts illustrated how a determined people evolved self-government from charters which had been granted essentially for trading or commercial purposes.

The ever-beckoning frontier fostered a feeling of independence and individualism which, even to this day, has been an outstanding mark on the American character. When things went badly in the more densely settled seaboard areas, there was always this wilderness where a man might start anew and prosper.

The framers could also look back upon the earlier attempts to form unions among the scattered settlements. As early as 1643, Massachusetts, New Haven, and Connecticut joined in a confederation for the primary purpose of protecting themselves against the Indians. In 1754 a more elaborate scheme for mutual protection and cooperation was advanced by Benjamin Franklin at the Albany Congress. Though neither of these plans proved successful, still the framers profited by their mistakes.

Most of the delegates to the Constitutional Convention had had years of experience in public affairs. They drew upon this intimate knowledge and upon the separate constitutions and experiences of the twelve states represented at Philadelphia. Such principles as separation of powers, limited government, bill of rights, checks and balances, and many others were common to all these state constitutions. Many of the practical problems of form and procedure had been worked out in the states over a period of years. Then, too, there were the Articles of Confederation from which to learn. To be sure, the Articles were lacking in several important areas of government; however, there was much that was good, and the framers incorporated these features into the new Constitution, without so much as changing a word.

Briefly then, we see that the Constitution as drafted by the Constitutional Convention was not only a carryover of certain English ideas and institutions, but was also a product of 150 years of colonial experience and evolution. It rightly deserves the praise accorded it by a former British prime minister who described it as "the most wonderful work ever struck off at a given time by the brain and purpose of man."

Chapter 2

Fundamental Principles In
Our Constitution

All governments rest upon a body of beliefs, ideas, and principles held in common by the people. The American government is no exception to this generalization. Principles are like foundation stones; they are sturdy, stable, and firmly rooted. Principles do not catch your eye or hold your interest long, but without them, the elaborate superstructure of government would quickly collapse.

American governments have these imposing superstructures—legislatures, executives, courts, and political parties that make the headlines. Supporting their functions, their duties, and actions, however, are fundamental principles or causes. In this chapter the principles underlying the American governmental system are discussed and defined. Recognizing these foundations will lead to better understanding of the operations of our several governments.

Consent of the Governed

The framers of the Constitution were steeped in the philosophy of John Locke and the social contract. From these sources and their own trying experiences came the belief that government was established by the people and is always accountable to the will of the people. Specialists in government often refer to this idea as *popular sovereignty.* Sovereignty is a French word meaning "highest or ultimate power." Applied to the American political scene it means that the people are the final judges of what their governments will be and how they shall operate.

Furthermore, it means that the people have consented to be governed by persons of their own choosing, under rules and regulations set down in written constitutions. This principle is clearly stated in the Preamble of the U.S. Constitution: "We the people of the United States...do ordain and establish this Constitution for the United States of America." Many of our state constitutions begin in a similar fashion. The principle has never been more nobly expressed than in the immortal words of President Abraham Lincoln at Gettysburg in 1863—"that government of the people, by the people, for the people shall not perish from the earth."

Limited Government

If the people are the ultimate sources of authority, then it follows that the governments they create are not all-powerful. The founding fathers, putting theory into practice, established limited governments possessing only those powers actually conferred upon them.

Under the United States Constitution, the national government was given definite powers. Most of these powers were listed in Article I, Section 8, though other powers are found in other articles of the Constitution. This listing or enumerating of powers is the basis of calling the national government a *government of enumerated powers.*

The Constitution also reserves certain powers to the states (Amendment 10), while still other political powers are retained by the people (Amendments 9 and 10).

Our state governments are also limited, even in those areas reserved to them by the United States Constitution. State constitutions impose limitations upon the exercise of governmental authority by their legislatures, courts, and executives. Article I, Section 10 of the federal Constitution also contains several restrictions, as do several of the amendments, on the exercise of state powers. Local governments are limited by state constitutions and state laws because they owe their existence to the state governments.

Governments in the United States have been established to aid and protect the people. It is the individual who counts, and government exists to further his or her well being. This ideal is quite different from the concept of the all-powerful government in fascist and communist countries, where the individual exists only to glorify and strengthen the power of the state.

Civil Rights

The framers of the Constitution believed that limited government could best be maintained by guaranteeing the people civil rights. A *right,* legally speaking, acts as a limitation upon the exercise of power. Thus large areas of human conduct were reserved for the people. These freedoms were protected against government interference by the national and state constitutions.

In the national Constitution, the first ten amendments, known as the Bill of Rights, contain the bulk of our civil rights. Other freedoms are guaranteed by the original Constitution and later amendments. Each state's constitution also contains a bill of rights applying to its inhabitants. Two sets of civil rights might prove confusing, but fortunately, the states' bills of rights are very similar to those of the federal Constitution.

Without going into detail or making an all-inclusive list, we can divide our civil rights into two broad categories:

(1) Rights relating to personal liberty:
    a. Freedom of speech, press, religion, assembly.
    b. Right to indictment by grand jury, trial by jury, right to counsel.
    c. Freedom from unreasonable search and seizures, freedom from self-incrimination.

(2) Rights relating to property:
    a. Due process of law.
    b. Just compensation, uniform taxation.

Rights of each individual are not absolute. No person has complete, unlimited use of all of his or her civil rights. For if such were the case, then total liberty for one person would impose limitations upon other persons. We cannot use our freedom of speech and press to slander or libel someone. We cannot use our freedom of religion to practice polygamy. The exercise of our rights depends upon the time, place, and reasonableness of the action. The courts are the final judges as to their legitimate use.

Separation of Powers

The early Americans were distrustful of one or a few individuals accumulating too much political power. In order to safeguard the liberties of the people, political authority was parceled out to many different people. Under the doctrine of *separation of powers,* certain authority is assigned to specific officers or agencies of the government. The Congress is given lawmaking powers, the President is given executive powers, and the judicial branch is delegated judicial powers. Within the legislative branch, the principle of *bicameralism* carries the doctrine still further. Bicameralism provides for a legislature with two separate, but equal, bodies or houses. State constitutions divide the powers in the same manner, and every state, with one exception, has a bicameral legislature.

Theoretically one branch of the government may not exercise powers given to another branch. In practice, however, there is no complete separation. For example, in vetoing laws passed by the Congress, the President engages in a legislative function. The doctrine of separation of powers is most clearly demonstrated by the fact that no executive official can be a member of the legislative or judicial branches at the same time.

Checks and Balances

Not only was political power divided by the framers, but they also gave each branch some degree of control over the other branches. The framers reasoned that the principle of *checks and balances* would prevent any one branch from ignoring or overpowering the other branches. For example, the President, or governor, may check the legislature by vetoing a certain measure. This action is balanced by the legislature's power to override the veto by an extraordinary vote. Or the judiciary may declare a law unconstitutional. This check is balanced by the President's power to appoint members to the courts and Congress's powers to fix the size and the jurisdiction of the courts.

We could select a number of such instances where a power exercised by one branch is, in some manner, checked or balanced by powers held by the other branches of our government.

Judicial Review

Judicial review refers to the action of a court in declaring an act of the legislature null and void, i.e., unconstitutional. No specific clause in the national Constitution confers this power on the courts. Very early in our history, state courts had exercised this function. In 1803, Chief Justice John Marshall of the U.S. Supreme Court declared part of an act of Congress unconstitutional in the famous case of *Marbury v. Madison.* Marshall found authority for judicial review in the fact that the Constitution was the supreme and highest law of the land. The courts, as special guardians of the Constitution, must prefer the Constitution to any other law whenever there is a conflict between the two. At the time the decision was announced, there were a number of persons who challenged the courts' authority, but the precedent was established. With the passage of time, the doctrine of judicial review has become a fundamental principle in our governmental system and was reaffirmed as recently as 1974 in the case of *United States v. Richard M. Nixon, President.*

Universal Adult Suffrage

When the Constitution was adopted, a relatively small percentage of the population enjoyed the privilege of participating in state or national elections. Negroes and women were excluded. In order to vote in some states, a person had to own a certain amount of property or pay a certain amount of taxes. A few states even had religious tests.

One by one these qualifications were eliminated. First to go were the religious tests, then property ownership, and finally tax-paying requirements. The Civil War resulted in the Fifteenth Amendment, which enfranchised Negroes. Fifty years later the Nineteenth Amendment was passed and women were given the right to vote, and recently the Twenty-Sixth Amendment lowered the voting age to 18. At the mid-point of the twentieth century, the United States had achieved what amounts to universal adult suffrage. That is, all citizens meeting minimum qualifications (residence, age) may exercise the privilege of voting in state and national elections. To be sure, not all persons care to exercise this privilege. Also, in some parts of the country the African-American citizen has not been able to exercise fully his legal rights. Nevertheless, the United States has far surpassed other nations of the world by permitting so many persons to vote under so few requirements.

Self-Government

Since the earliest settlements in the New World, Americans have demonstrated the will and the ability to govern themselves. Our constitutions reflect the belief that there are capable, hard-working, honest citizens who consider it an honor to serve their fellow Americans. The founding fathers provided popularly elected officials for one house of Congress. The presidency and vice presidency were to be filled by an indirect election method. Their faith in self-government has been amply justified by our nation's history. The Senate, once selected by state legislatures, became a popularly elected body under the Seventeenth Amendment. The indirect election of the president and vice president has become obsolete for all practical purposes.

The states practiced self-government long before the national Constitution was adopted. The major executive officials and both houses of the legislature are elected in all states. In addition, many states provide for the popular election of judges. Thousands of public officials are elected by the people to serve in the local governments. Self-government is so much a part of the American tradition that countless essential activities are carried on by townships, counties, cities, and other local units of government.

Federalism

The United States of America is often identified as a *federal state*. This simply means that there is a division of governmental power between the central or national government and regional or state governments. Neither government has all the powers. Some powers, such as foreign commerce, the national government alone possesses. Other powers, such as marriage and divorce, the states possess exclusively, while both federal and state governments possess other powers, such as taxation. The United States Constitution establishes the general areas set aside for each of the units of government. Both governments, however, operate directly on the individual. Though independent of each other, the states and the national government are cooperative partners within the federal system.

It was the clear intent of the framers to establish federalism within the Constitution by creating a national government of enumerated powers. The principle was reaffirmed by the addition of the Tenth Amendment, which states:

> THE POWERS NOT DELEGATED TO THE UNITED STATES BY THE CONSTITUTION, NOR PROHIBITED BY IT TO THE STATES, ARE RESERVED TO THE STATES RESPECTIVELY, OR TO THE PEOPLE.

Representative Democracy

A true democracy is a government in which the people directly control and exercise the powers of government. Our New England towns practiced this type of democracy many years ago. All the townspeople entitled to vote would gather at the town hall and personally vote on the policies and operations of their government. True democracy works well in a small community, but applying it to an entire nation would be impossible. So in the United States we have what might best be called a *representative democracy*. The people choose representatives—congressmen, state legislators, presidents, and governors—and instruct these persons to act for them in the enactment of laws and in policy-making. This is a republican form of government. But the ultimate control rests with the people, and this fact makes the United States and the fifty states democracies.

In the United States, however, the conception of democracy in the minds of the people goes beyond a mere description of a form of government. In our thinking, democracy is more a way of life than a mere mechanical or political arrangement. When we think of democracy, we think of civil rights, political freedoms, limited government, judicial review, and all the other principles mentioned earlier. In addition, we think of individualism, right to property, private initiative, and freedom of opportunity as being part of the democratic tradition.

Most of us would have difficulty putting our thoughts on democracy into writing. There would be a variety of meanings and perhaps few definitions would be the same. Still, we would probably agree on the hard core of principles outlined here. This variety of meaning would only give added strength to another bulwark of American democracy—a diversity of opinion and an antagonism toward conformity.

Chapter 3

How to Understand Our Constitutional System

The United States Constitution has been formally amended twenty-seven times. Ten of these amendments were approved within a few years after the adoption of the original document and the remaining sixteen have been ratified over a period of nearly 205 years.

Our instrument of government, conceived in the spirit of the eighteenth century, is still working exceedingly well as we approach the twenty-first century. No other nation in the world has retained its written constitution as long as has the United States; nor have any of the fifty states.

Why has our national Constitution remained so stable and workable while other nations and states have amended, revised, and adopted numerous constitutions? The answer lies in the fact that our national Constitution contains general principles and confers broad grants of power to the various branches of government. The framers omitted details and petty matters which, history demonstrates, have a tendency to paralyze growth and development. The framers had faith in the men who would occupy the positions of trust and responsibility in the government. That faith has been well rewarded throughout our history.

Strictly speaking, the original document with its twenty-seven amendments is *the Constitution.* In the broad sense, our Constitution extends beyond the formal writings. Our "living Constitution" includes lasting enactments of Congress, important actions by the chief executive, and significant decisions by our courts. Our constitutional system has also grown as a result of customs and traditions that have developed around institutions and officers. In this chapter we will review the expansion of our documentary constitution into what might easily be called our *living Constitution.*

Expansion by Acts of Congress

The framers of the Constitution created the broad outlines of government. They left to Congress a multitude of powers from which it could create the details. In the past 205 years Congress has enacted thousands of laws, most of which have had only temporary importance. Yet a number of enactments stand out because of their fundamental importance. Congress is given the broad power to create "inferior courts" to the Supreme Court. The Constitution does not say how many courts, where they are to be located, what their jurisdiction is to be, or how many judges are to sit. These details have been left to Congress. Thus in 1789 Congress passed the Judiciary Act which established a system of lower federal courts. In part, this statute remains the basis of our present-day court structure.

A few indirect references are made in the Constitution to "executive departments." By law, Congress has established, over a period of years, an enormous executive branch consisting of fourteen departments and a number of commissions, boards, and agencies— these latter completely unknown to the Constitution. Are not the Department of Agriculture or the Interstate Commerce Commission essential parts of our constitutional system today?

Congress is given power to regulate commerce. The Constitution does not say how, when, or by what means. Yet the Sherman Anti-Trust Act, the Clayton Act, the Fair Labor Standards Act, and the Taft-Hartley Act illustrate the importance of statutes in the development of our "living Constitution."

Elaboration by Executive Policy

The President and his subordinates in the executive branch are also involved in constitutional development. Congress enacts statutes, but the President, operating through his administrators, enforces the laws. Whatever interpretation they give to a law, in effect, changes that law. The administrators do their best, of course, to give the law the meaning that Congress intends it to have. In some cases, the vagueness of the law leaves the executive branch no choice but to exercise a large measure of discretion.

In the twentieth century, Congress, of necessity, is delegating to the executive branch more power to fill in the details. Our highly complicated society prevents Congress from foreseeing every possible implication and effect of the actual operation of the law. Therefore Congress enacts general standards that guide and limit the executive branch. Our entire program of reciprocal trade operates in this fashion. Congress permits tariffs to be raised or lowered to a maximum of 50 percent. The executive branch determines the precise change within these limits.

A former president established a precedent in our constitutional system. When the House Un-American Activities Committee ordered former President Harry S Truman to appear before it in 1953, he refused on the ground that such an appearance would violate the principle of separation of powers, even though he was no longer an official in the government. Thereafter the Committee abandoned its attempt to call the former president to testify.

In January, 1981, in one of his first decisions as President, Ronald W. Reagan issued an executive order decontrolling crude oil, gasoline, and propane prices without concurring congressional action or legislation. In like fashion, in the first few weeks of his administration in 1993, President Bill Clinton lifted the executive ban on abortions performed at federal hospitals.

On the other hand, a president may not arbitrarily establish a policy and be completely immune from the authority of other branches of government. For example, in 1952 President Truman interpreted the Constitution as giving him power to seize the steel mills then idled by strikes. The judicial branch, however, refused to follow his interpretation and ordered the government to return control of the mills to their private owners.

Judicial Interpretation

The judiciary enjoys a special and privileged position in our American system of government. It is the final arbiter of constitutional questions. The Congress may pass laws and the President may enforce them, but the courts must apply these laws to specific cases. The meaning that the courts place on the various phrases and terms in the Constitution has had a decided influence over the course of history. Because the court decided that states could be sued in the federal courts, that Negroes were not citizens, and that a tax on income was a direct tax, the Eleventh, Fourteenth, and Sixteenth Amendments had to be proposed and adopted. This is not to say that once the court has decided a principle one way, it will never change. Actual events tell a different story. Judges die, and judges with different viewpoints take their place. For example, in 1923 the Supreme Court declared unconstitutional a minimum wage law for women. In 1937, with new personnel, the Supreme Court upheld a similar minimum wage law.

An outstanding example of how the courts "make" constitutional law is offered by a case in 1860. In this case, the governor of Ohio refused to comply with the request of the governor of Kentucky to return a fugitive from Ohio. Kentucky appealed to the federal courts because the Constitution stated that such a fugitive "shall, on demand..., be delivered up...." (Article 4, Section 2). The Supreme Court interpreted "shall" to mean "may." Thus, instead of a mandatory duty on the governor, it merely made his action a moral duty to return a fugitive criminal. Therefore, without an amendment, our Constitution was changed by judicial interpretation.

Expansion by Custom, Usage, and Tradition

Time and tradition are always at work on institutions. A practice long used eventually becomes so encrusted with acceptability that many persons actually believe the practice is part of our constitutional system. Take political parties, for example. The operations of our government today cannot be understood without knowledge of how parties work. Yet many of the founding fathers, among them George Washington, foresaw only troubles and ruination if political parties gained a foothold in our governmental system. Parties did develop and were completely outside the scope of our laws for decades. Even today, national conventions and national committees are largely independent of legal regulation.

Custom and usage have also changed the function of the electoral college. The framers intended that the electors should exercise their own judgment when casting their electoral votes. Today, as for decades, the electors are merely agents of the political parties. Imagine the uproar from the millions of voters who supported President Clinton if a majority of the electors had cast their ballots for Ross Perot in 1992.

Our executive cabinet, as an institution, is another creature of custom. Perhaps the most widely publicized custom was the so-called third-term tradition. No person, custom decreed, should be elected for a third term as president. The tradition lasted for 150 years, until Franklin D. Roosevelt was elected to a third term in 1940 and a fourth term in 1944. This incident illustrates that a custom or tradition is not law. Custom depends upon the widespread, almost universal, acceptance of the people for its enforcement. The third-term tradition lacked this support in 1940 and 1944, but shortly thereafter the "tradition" was firmly implanted in our constitutional law with the adoption of the Twenty-Second Amendment, forbidding a third term of office to our chief executive.

In summation, we see how the term "constitution" can be used with two different meanings. Most often it is used to designate a written fundamental law of special importance. This document outlines the structure of government, fixes the powers of the branches of government, guarantees liberties and rights, and lays down the general principles of procedure in applying government. This is a constitution in its narrowest sense. On the other hand, the term "constitution" refers not simply to documentary fundamental law, but to an array of principles, statutes, usages, and interpretations clustering around such a law, many of which are not even set down in writing. This is a constitution in its broadest sense—a living constitution.

Chapter 4

The United States Constitution

A review of the history and principles of the Constitution sets the stage for a detailed discussion of these provisions. Intelligent discussion of our constitutional system demands frequent reference to principles in order to explain or elaborate certain practices.

In this chapter each Article and Amendment to the Constitution is divided into its basic elements—sections and clauses. Each section and clause is appropriately headed by a title describing its content. The constitutional wording is followed by a discussion of the meaning and actual practices of the clause or phrase under consideration. As a further aid to the development and clarity of the meaning, a number of examples taken directly from actual court cases are used. We begin, therefore, with the Preamble of the United States Constitution.

The Preamble

WE THE PEOPLE OF THE UNITED STATES, IN ORDER TO FORM A MORE PERFECT UNION, ESTABLISH JUSTICE, INSURE DOMESTIC TRANQUILITY, PROVIDE FOR THE COMMON DEFENSE, PROMOTE THE GENERAL WELFARE, AND SECURE THE BLESSINGS OF LIBERTY TO OURSELVES AND OUR POSTERITY, DO ORDAIN AND ESTABLISH THIS CONSTITUTION FOR THE UNITED STATES OF AMERICA.

The Preamble is a statement containing the reasons for drafting the Constitution and the purposes of the new government. The

Preamble does not confer any power upon any branch or agency of the national government. A person cannot go into a federal court and claim any right under the Preamble. Even though it confers no rights or powers, the Preamble is often used to illustrate the origin, scope, and purposes of the Constitution. Above all, the Preamble makes certain that the Constitution rests upon the consent of the people, rather than upon any other source of authority, including the states.

Article I

The Legislative Branch

Section 1   The Congress

ALL LEGISLATIVE POWERS HEREIN GRANTED SHALL BE VESTED IN A CONGRESS OF THE UNITED STATES, WHICH SHALL CONSIST OF A SENATE AND HOUSE OF REPRESENTATIVES.

This section establishes two great principles of American Constitutional law. The first principle is that the national government is one of *enumerated powers.* "All legislative powers herein granted" means that the federal government may exercise those powers that are listed or enumerated in Section 8, together with such powers as may reasonably be implied from a specific power or result from a whole mass of delegated powers. For example, Congress is given the specific power of coining money and regulating its value. From this expressed power, the courts have implied that Congress has the power to incorporate a bank—something which was not, and still is not, definitely stated in the Constitution. Congress, however, cannot do anything it desires to do; there are limits to what may be implied from a specific power. For example, the power to admit territories as new states did not give Congress the implied power of requiring Oklahoma to keep its capital at Guthrie for five years against its will.

The other principle established by this section is a *bicameral legislature.* Two separate yet equal legislative bodies were created—the Senate and the House of Representatives.

Section 2   The House of Representatives

Clause 1. <u>Elections and Terms of Office</u>

> THE HOUSE OF REPRESENTATIVES SHALL BE COMPOSED OF
> MEMBERS CHOSEN EVERY SECOND YEAR BY THE PEOPLE OF THE
> SEVERAL STATES, AND THE ELECTORS IN EACH STATE SHALL HAVE
> THE QUALIFICATIONS REQUISITE FOR ELECTORS OF THE MOST
> NUMEROUS BRANCH OF THE STATE LEGISLATURE.

This clause established a two-year term of office for members of the House of Representatives. They are elected every even-numbered year (i.e., 1996, 1998, 2000, etc.) on the first Tuesday after the first Monday in November. The electors, or voters, become eligible to vote for members of the House if they meet the qualifications set up by the states for voting in elections for state representatives. This means that the individual states establish the requirements, creating the possibility of differences from state to state.

In the context of an "anti-incumbent" movement during the 1990s, fifteen states adopted initiatives that set limits to the number of terms congressmen or women and state officials could serve. State courts had upheld limits on state officials, but a federal district judge in the state of Washington ruled in February, 1994 that congressional term limits were unconstitutional. Judge William L. Dwyer's rationale was that term limits were not required as a qualification for congressional candidacy by the Constitution (see next clause). Proponents of term limits promised to take appeals of this decision all the way to the Supreme Court.

Even though the qualifications for voters are defined by state law, the *right* to vote for members of Congress comes from the national Constitution. Therefore Congress can pass, and has passed, certain laws regulating the conduct of federal elections. Federal courts, for example, have held that stuffing the ballot boxes in a federal election is a crime punishable by federal law. Intimidating Negroes or others by threats or violence also interferes with this right to vote for federal offices.

Clause 2. <u>Qualifications for Members</u>

NO PERSON SHALL BE A REPRESENTATIVE WHO SHALL NOT
HAVE ATTAINED TO THE AGE OF TWENTY-FIVE YEARS, AND BEEN
SEVEN YEARS A CITIZEN OF THE UNITED STATES, AND WHO SHALL
NOT, WHEN ELECTED, BE AN INHABITANT OF THE STATE IN WHICH
HE SHALL BE CHOSEN.

These are purely legal qualifications. A Representative must be twenty-five years of age, at least seven years a citizen of the United States, and a citizen of his or her state. A person who does not meet those requirements would not be allowed to participate in the business of the House until he or she qualified. However, it is the exceptional person who does not already possess these qualifications before becoming a candidate. In fact, it is highly unlikely that a political party would support a candidate who did not meet them. Few naturalized citizens are elected to Congress in this era, though D. S. Sound, a Hindu, born in India, was elected in 1956. Nor are there many younger persons.

Interestingly, a Representative need only be a citizen of his state, and not necessarily a resident of the district that he represents. That is to say, it is legal for a person living in Philadelphia to run for Representative in a western Pennsylvania district. We know, of course, that he would not have much of a chance of being elected, because one of our political traditions expects a Representative to be a resident of his district. This tradition contrasts strikingly with that of England, where, for example, a man from London may be elected from a district on the Scottish border.

Clause 3. <u>Apportionment of Representatives</u>

<u>REPRESENTATIVES AND DIRECT TAXES SHALL BE</u>
<u>APPORTIONED AMONG THE SEVERAL STATES WHICH MAY BE</u>
<u>INCLUDED WITHIN THIS UNION, ACCORDING TO THEIR RESPECTIVE</u>
<u>NUMBERS, WHICH SHALL BE DETERMINED BY ADDING TO THE</u>
<u>WHOLE NUMBER OF FREE PERSONS, INCLUDING THOSE BOUND TO</u>

SERVICE FOR A TERM OF YEARS, AND EXCLUDING INDIANS NOT TAXED, THREE FIFTHS OF ALL OTHER PERSONS. THE ACTUAL ENUMERATION SHALL BE MADE WITHIN THREE YEARS AFTER THE FIRST MEETING OF THE CONGRESS OF THE UNITED STATES, AND WITHIN EVERY SUBSEQUENT TERM OF TEN YEARS, IN SUCH MANNER AS THEY SHALL BY LAW DIRECT, THE NUMBER OF REPRESENTATIVES SHALL NOT EXCEED ONE FOR EVERY THIRTY THOUSAND, BUT EACH STATE SHALL HAVE AT LEAST ONE REPRESENTATIVE; AND UNTIL SUCH ENUMERATION SHALL BE MADE, THE STATE OF NEW HAMPSHIRE SHALL BE ENTITLED TO CHOOSE THREE, MASSACHUSETTS EIGHT, RHODE ISLAND AND PROVIDENCE PLANTATIONS ONE, CONNECTICUT FIVE, NEW YORK SIX, NEW JERSEY FOUR, PENNSYLVANIA EIGHT, DELAWARE ONE, MARYLAND SIX, VIRGINIA TEN, NORTH CAROLINA FIVE, SOUTH CAROLINA FIVE AND GEORGIA THREE.

The underlined portion of this clause has become obsolete because of Amendments XIII, XIV, and XVI. The Thirteenth Amendment outlawed slavery, the Fourteenth changed the method of apportioning Representatives, and the Sixteenth permitted taxes on income without reference to population. The original sentence had been included in the Constitution as a compromise between northern and southern states over the question of representation and taxation.

Indians have a special status in American government. By law, Congress extended U.S. citizenship to all Native Americans (Indians, Aleuts, Eskimos) on and off the 299 reservations. Indians have the same rights, privileges, and obligations as any other citizen. However, on the reservations, which are lands set aside for Indian use and held in trust by the national government, Indian tribal councils manage their own affairs subject to ultimate supervision by Congress and the Bureau of Indian Affairs in the Department of the Interior. States may extend the voting franchise to reservation Indians, but other state laws, especially those dealing with taxes, may only apply to the reservations if Congress specifically sanctions them.

This clause also provides the basis for our decennial (ten year) census. The number of Representatives to which each state was entitled was purely temporary until a census could be taken. The original ratio, one Representative for each 30,000 persons, would be completely unworkable today. In 1929 Congress established a limit of 435 to the size of the House of Representatives (this can be changed by any Congress, but none have done so). The 435 Representatives are apportioned, or distributed, among the states according to their population. Roughly speaking, the 1990 census resulted in a ratio of one Representative for every 571,900 persons. The larger states have more Representatives than the less populous states; however, each state is entitled to at least one Representative, even though that state may not have the necessary number of inhabitants. For example, Wyoming had only 453,588 inhabitants in 1990, yet it is entitled to one Representative.

If the total number of Representatives remains fixed at 435 and our total population, as well as various states' populations increase, then it means that some states will lose Representatives. The 1990 census showed that Florida gained 3,190,965 in population. This tremendous expansion entitled Florida to four additional Representatives. Some other states, though increasing in population, did not gain as rapidly as had Florida. Thus, they had to lose seats— for example, Michigan lost two, Pennsylvania, two, and Kentucky, one. Every ten years this reshuffling takes place—some states gain, some lose, while others remain the same. The 1990 apportionment resulted in nineteen congressional seats exchanged among twenty-one states; primarily, the East and Midwest lost districts to the South and far West. The exact method of distributing the seats among the states in a fair and equitable manner involves the use of a complex mathematical formula. The Bureau of the Census computes each state's apportionment, which then becomes law unless Congress changes the formula.

After the national government informs the states how many Representatives they are entitled to, it is the responsibility of the state legislatures to divide the states into the necessary number of districts.

This is called *redistricting* and often involves bitter controversies between the political parties. Usually the party in control of the state legislature cuts up the state in such a way as to spread its own strength in as many districts as possible, while at the same time confining the strength of the opposition party into as few districts as possible. This practice is often referred to as *gerrymandering.* Supreme Court decisions, beginning with *Baker v. Carr* (1962) and *Wesberry v. Sanders* (1964), require state legislatures to make districts as equal in population as possible.

If the state's delegation is increased, it may either create new districts or elect the new Representatives "at large," that is, by all the voters of the state. If a state's quota is reduced, however, it must either redistrict or else all Representatives will be elected on an at-large basis.

Clause 4. Vacancies in the House

WHEN VACANCIES HAPPEN IN THE REPRESENTATION FROM ANY STATE, THE EXECUTIVE AUTHORITY THEREOF SHALL ISSUE WRITS OF ELECTION TO FILL SUCH VACANCIES.

This clause gives the governor the authority to call an election in order to fill a vacancy in any district within the state. Unless the unexpired term is rather lengthy—one year or more—the governor usually does not order a special election because the regular election occurs every two years. An election, even in one district, costs a considerable sum of money.

Clause 5. The Speaker of the House and Impeachment

THE HOUSE OF REPRESENTATIVES SHALL CHOOSE THEIR SPEAKER AND OTHER OFFICERS; AND SHALL HAVE THE SOLE POWER OF IMPEACHMENT.

The Speaker of the House is the presiding officer. He is a very important and powerful member of the House of Representatives.

Technically, he is elected by members of the House, but in reality he is selected by the majority party. Each party puts up a candidate and naturally the party with the most members in the House will elect its candidate. Some of the duties and powers of the Speaker include: recognizing members for debate, interpreting rules of parliamentary procedure, appointing special committees, keeping order in the House, and signing bills. Necessarily, the Speaker is a leader of his political party.

The power of impeachment is the first step in a two-step process. Impeachment means accusation, that is, preferring charges. In 1974, the House gave its Judiciary Committee the responsibility of drafting the impeachment articles against President Richard M. Nixon. The House of Representatives accuses, or impeaches. The next step is trying the accused, and that is done by the Senate. A majority vote, a quorum being present, is required for impeachment. Only after a person is found guilty by the Senate is he removed from office.

Section 3   The Senate

Clause 1. Election of Senators

> THE SENATE OF THE UNITED STATES SHALL BE COMPOSED OF
> TWO SENATORS FROM EACH STATE, CHOSEN BY THE LEGISLATURE
> THEREOF, FOR SIX YEARS; AND EACH SENATOR SHALL HAVE ONE
> VOTE.

The underlined portion of this clause has been replaced by the Seventeenth Amendment; that is, since 1915, Senators are chosen by direct popular election in each state.

This clause recalls the disagreements within the Constitutional Convention of 1787. You will remember that one part of the famous Connecticut Compromise gave the small states equality of membership in one of the houses of the legislature. This clause provides for that equality. Each state, no matter how large or small, is entitled to two Senators. In the early period of our history the differences among the states' with respect to population were important but not substantial. The tremendous growth of the country, however, has brought about vast population inequalities. For example, according to the 1990 census, Wyoming has a population of 453,588 yet it has the same number of Senators as the state of New York with its 17,990,455 population. The differential, of course, would be greater in the case of California. It is quite unlikely that this equality provision will ever be changed, because it serves as a protection to the less populous states in the twentieth century, as it did for the smaller states in the eighteenth century.

Little needs to be said concerning the other points in this clause. One Senator, one vote. He cannot transfer it to anyone else. He serves for six years, much longer than the term of office of a Representative, an advantage that gives Senators more prestige and greater opportunity for reelection.

Clause 2. Rotation of Terms of Office for Senators

> IMMEDIATELY AFTER THEY SHALL BE ASSEMBLED IN CONSEQUENCE OF THE FIRST ELECTION, THEY SHALL BE DIVIDED AS EQUALLY AS MAY BE INTO THREE CLASSES, THE SEATS OF THE SENATORS OF THE FIRST CLASS SHALL BE VACATED AT THE EXPIRATION OF THE SECOND YEAR, OF THE SECOND CLASS AT THE EXPIRATION OF THE FOURTH YEAR, AND OF THE THIRD CLASS AT THE EXPIRATION OF THE SIXTH YEAR, SO THAT ONE THIRD MAY BE CHOSEN EVERY SECOND YEAR; AND IF VACANCIES HAPPEN BY RESIGNATION, OR OTHERWISE, DURING THE RECESS OF THE LEGISLATURE OF ANY STATE, THE EXECUTIVE THEREOF MAY MAKE TEMPORARY APPOINTMENTS UNTIL THE NEXT MEETING OF THE LEGISLATURE, WHICH SHALL THEN FILL SUCH VACANCIES.

This clause provides the Senate with an overlapping membership. Only one-third of the Senators come up for election at the same time. This leaves two-thirds of the Senate always in office. This is the basis of the Senate contention that it is a continuous body, having been in session since 1789.

The division of the Senate into the three classes was an arbitrary arrangement. However, it was planned so that no state would have two Senators up for election in the same year. This sometimes happens because a vacancy might have been created by the death of an incumbent Senator. Such an election would be to fill the unexpired term and not for a full six-year term.

The underlined portion of this clause has been altered somewhat by the Seventeenth Amendment and the requirement of a popular election. Temporary appointments may be made by the governor acting under authority granted to him by his state legislature. A Senator appointed in this manner is entitled to and does enjoy all the rights, privileges, and compensation accorded to elected Senators. Such a Senator serves until such time as an election is held to fill the unexpired term.

Clause 3. <u>Qualifications for Senators</u>

> NO PERSON SHALL BE A SENATOR WHO SHALL NOT HAVE ATTAINED TO THE AGE OF THIRTY YEARS, AND BEEN NINE YEARS A CITIZEN OF THE UNITED STATES, AND WHO SHALL NOT, WHEN ELECTED, BE AN INHABITANT OF THAT STATE FOR WHICH HE SHALL BE CHOSEN.

These are purely legal qualifications and it is easily seen that they are not significant in contemporary politics. More important to a potential candidate are what we might call "political qualifications." That is to say, does he live in the right part of the state, does she belong to the right party for that state, is he friendly with the party leaders, does she have a large popular following, can he afford to spend time and money on campaigns? It is safe to say that a young man or woman of thirty, newly arrived in the state or country, has a very poor chance of winning such high office.

This clause also ties in with our comments on the House of Representatives being the judge of the elections, returns, and qualifications of its members. The Senate also decides these qualifications when required to do so.

Clause 4. Presiding Officer of the Senate

> THE VICE-PRESIDENT OF THE UNITED STATES SHALL BE
> PRESIDENT OF THE SENATE, BUT SHALL HAVE NO VOTE, UNLESS
> THEY BE EQUALLY DIVIDED.

This clause names an executive official, the Vice-President, as the presiding officer of the Senate. He is not a member of the Senate, and therefore cannot vote except to break a tie. The Vice-President has much less influence and control over the Senate than the Speaker of the House has over his membership. As an "outsider" the Vice-President makes his influence felt by means of his personality and close friendships. The Speaker's powers come from House rules, customs, and party loyalty, as well as personal popularity.

Clause 5. Other Officers of the Senate

> THE SENATE SHALL CHOOSE THEIR OTHER OFFICERS, AND
> ALSO A PRESIDENT PRO TEMPORE, IN THE ABSENCE OF THE VICE-
> PRESIDENT, OR WHEN HE SHALL EXERCISE THE OFFICE OF PRESIDENT
> OF THE UNITED STATES.

The president pro tempore is selected by the majority party. That is, the political party that controls at least fifty-one seats, excluding the Vice-President, selects one of its members, usually the man with the longest continuous service in his party in the Senate, and nominates him for the office. The Senate elects as a body, but since the majority party has the most votes, its candidate is inevitably elected. The President pro tem, as he is most often called, can vote and debate on any and all measures, even while acting as the presiding officer, because he is a member of the Senate.

Clause 6. Trial of Impeachments

> THE SENATE SHALL HAVE THE SOLE POWER TO TRY ALL
> IMPEACHMENTS. WHEN SITTING FOR THAT PURPOSE, THEY SHALL
> BE ON OATH OR AFFIRMATION, WHEN THE PRESIDENT OF THE

UNITED STATES IS TRIED, THE CHIEF JUSTICE SHALL PRESIDE: AND
NO PERSON SHALL BE CONVICTED WITHOUT THE CONCURRENCE
OF TWO THIRDS OF THE MEMBERS PRESENT.

This is the second part of the impeachment process. The House of Representatives impeaches, or accuses; the Senate acts as a court to try the accused.

Two-thirds of the Senators present must vote in favor of the charges in order for the person to be convicted. In our history under the Constitution, the House has impeached only fifteen civil officers of the United States. Military personnel and members of Congress do not come under the impeachment process. Of the fifteen impeached, the Senate has convicted only seven, each a judge in the lower federal courts. Supreme Court Justice Samuel Chase was impeached in 1805 and President Andrew Johnson in 1868, but the Senate failed to convict either one. When the President of the United States is tried, the Chief Justice of the Supreme Court presides over the proceedings. In all other cases the Vice-President, as president of the Senate, presides. It is unclear who presides in the case of the trial of the Vice-President, but constitutional authorities tend to believe the Chief Justice would be the appropriate presiding officer.

Past practice had the entire Senate participating in the often long drawn out proceedings of an impeachment trial (questioning witnesses, authenticating evidence, referencing documents, etc.). A trial could tie up the Senate for weeks, even months. To avoid this possibility, the Senate in 1986 set up a special committee to hear the detailed evidence and report its findings to the full membership. Closing arguments would be heard in open session, discussion and debate would occur privately but a vote would be taken publicly on each item of the impeachment. In 1986, Federal District Court Judge Harry Claiborne was tried and convicted in this manner and removed from office. A similar committee tribunal was used in 1989 in the impeachment trials of District Court Judges Alcee L. Hastings and Walter L. Nixon, Jr., both convicted and removed from office. Judge Hastings appealed his conviction on grounds that the full Senate should have been involved in all the proceedings, and a District Court agreed. The Senate appealed this ruling on grounds that the judicial branch has no jurisdiction over impeachments, a contention upheld by the appellate court and Supreme Court.

Clause 7. Penalties for Conviction

> JUDGMENT IN CASES OF IMPEACHMENT SHALL NOT EXCEED FURTHER THAN REMOVAL FROM OFFICE, AND DISQUALIFICATION TO HOLD AND ENJOY ANY OFFICE OF HONOR, TRUST OR PROFIT UNDER THE UNITED STATES: BUT THE PARTY CONVICTED SHALL NEVERTHELESS BE LIABLE AND SUBJECT TO INDICTMENT, TRIAL, JUDGEMENT AND PUNISHMENT, ACCORDING TO LAW.

This means that the only punishment that a person suffers because of conviction is the removal from his office and a possible lifetime ban on holding any other public office in the U.S. government. Furthermore, the President cannot pardon anybody who has been convicted by impeachment.

Judge Hastings keeps adding to the interpretation of this section by his election in 1992 to the House of Representatives (the body that had impeached him in 1989). No one raised constitutional questions on his holding office.

Although Congress cannot add punishment to a conviction, it does not mean that a person necessarily escapes further legal prosecution. If a person has violated a law of the United States, he may be tried in the regular courts for that crime, and if convicted, be subject to the same punishment as any other criminal.

Section 4   Elections and Meetings of Congress

Clause 1. Times of Election for Members of Congress

> THE TIMES, PLACES AND MANNER OF HOLDING ELECTIONS FOR SENATORS AND REPRESENTATIVES SHALL BE PRESCRIBED IN EACH STATE BY THE LEGISLATURE THEREOF; BUT THE CONGRESS MAY AT ANY TIME BY LAW MAKE OR ALTER SUCH REGULATIONS, EXCEPT AS TO THE PLACES OF CHOOSING SENATORS.

Although Congress possessed the power to make regulations concerning federal elections, it did not exercise this power until 1842. Since that time, Congress has passed numerous laws affecting the times, places, and manner of holding federal elections. The Seventeenth Amendment gives Congress power over the underlined portion of this clause. By law, federal elections occur on the first Tuesday after the first Monday in November in the even-numbered years. All states follow this rule since Maine voted to elect congressmen in November beginning in 1960.

Representatives are to be elected from districts that, since the *Baker v. Carr* decision in 1962, may be attacked in the courts on grounds of inequality or unrepresentativeness. Congress can prohibit certain fraudulent practices such as bribery or stuffing the ballot boxes. These corrupt practices are also banned at primaries where candidates for federal offices are to be nominated. In recent years, Congress and the courts have intervened more directly in the state elections.

Clause 2. Meetings of Congress

THE CONGRESS SHALL ASSEMBLE AT LEAST ONCE EACH YEAR, AND SUCH MEETING SHALL BE ON THE FIRST MONDAY IN DECEMBER, UNLESS THEY SHALL BY LAW APPOINT A DIFFERENT DAY.

The Twentieth Amendment, approved in 1933, has provided a different time of meeting—January 3 of every year. This clause has been amended out of the Constitution.

Section 5   Proceedings of Congress

Clause 1. Judges of Own Members

EACH HOUSE SHALL BE THE JUDGE OF THE ELECTIONS, RETURNS AND QUALIFICATIONS OF ITS OWN MEMBERS, AND A MAJORITY OF EACH SHALL CONSTITUTE A QUORUM TO DO BUSINESS; BUT A SMALLER NUMBER MAY ADJOURN FROM DAY TO DAY, AND MAY BE AUTHORIZED TO COMPEL THE ATTENDANCE OF

ABSENT MEMBERS, IN SUCH MANNER, AND UNDER SUCH PENALTIES
AS EACH HOUSE MAY PROVIDE.

We have already mentioned the legal qualifications that each member of Congress is required to have. Each house has the right to satisfy itself that every member of its body meets these legal qualifications and also is a legally, fairly elected, and proper person to participate in the national legislature. In the past, each house has refused to seat a person even though he met all the constitutional requirements and had been legally elected. For example, the Senate refused to seat Brigham N. Roberts of Utah in 1901 because he practiced polygamy. During World War I, Victor L. Berger was twice refused his seat in the House of Representatives because of his open opposition to the war and to the drafting of men. However, in 1969 the Supreme Court ruled in the case involving New York Congressman Adam Clayton Powell's exclusion from the House that Congress cannot require any other qualification than is set forth in the Constitution. Yet each house still has the power to determine the validity of a member's election.

New Hampshire authorities were unable to certify officially a winner of the 1974 U.S. Senate contest. After a year of fruitless discussion, the Senate declared the seat vacant and ordered a special election. Significantly, the Senate also authorized the former incumbent senator (who had decided not to run for reelection) to remain in the Senate so as to assure New Hampshire its rightful, legal representation. In order for the House of Representatives to transact business there would have to be 218 members physically present, even though not all of them would vote on a particular matter. In the Senate, it would necessitate fifty-one members in attendance for a quorum.

Clause 2. Disciplining Members

EACH HOUSE MAY DETERMINE THE RULES OF ITS PROCEEDINGS, PUNISH ITS MEMBERS FOR DISORDERLY BEHAVIOR, AND, WITH THE CONCURRENCE OF TWO THIRDS, EXPEL A MEMBER.

Each house has established a long list of rules to enable it to carry on business efficiently and effectively. These rules may be changed at any time by a vote of the appropriate chamber. Any infraction of these rules, as well as general disorderly behavior, may be punished by a vote of the respective houses.

Members of Congress do not come under the impeachment provisions of the Constitution. The only way they may be removed from office before the expiration of their term is by expulsion. A two-thirds vote is necessary to expel a member. Therefore it is easily understood why more persons have been refused admittance than have been expelled from Congress.

Clause 3. <u>Records of Legislative Proceedings</u>

> EACH HOUSE SHALL KEEP A JOURNAL OF ITS PROCEEDINGS, AND FROM TIME TO TIME PUBLISH THE SAME, EXCEPTING SUCH PARTS AS MAY IN THEIR JUDGMENT REQUIRE SECRECY; AND YEAS AND NAYS OF THE MEMBERS OF EITHER HOUSE ON ANY QUESTION SHALL, AT THE DESIRE OF ONE FIFTH OF THOSE PRESENT, BE ENTERED ON THE JOURNAL.

The *journal* is the official record of each house. Actually, the journal is a rather sketchy account of the daily proceedings; it merely contains the essential highlights of the day's activities. Each house has its own journal; in fact, the Senate has four journals, one for each of the types of business it transacts.

There is another document, called the *Congressional Record,* which contains a full stenographic account of all the happenings in each house. It is the *Record* to which we refer for debates, speeches, and other daily occurrences even though some material may be printed that was not said on the floor of the chamber.

This clause also brings out another interesting fact about Congress. Most legislation is passed by voice votes. Therefore no record is made of how each individual Senator or Representative voted on an issue. Only when one-fifth of a quorum requests a "yea or nay" vote, will we find out how each congressman votes. A "yea or nay" vote is commonly called a "roll-call" or "record vote."

Clause 4. Temporary Adjournment of Congress

> NEITHER HOUSE, DURING THE SESSION OF CONGRESS, SHALL, WITHOUT THE CONSENT OF THE OTHER, ADJOURN FOR MORE THAN THREE DAYS, NOR TO ANY OTHER PLACE THAN THAT IN WHICH THE TWO HOUSES SHALL BE SITTING.

This provision simply means that the House of Representatives and the Senate must meet in the same place. If one house could adjourn whenever it pleased, then its absence could possibly stop the entire legislative machinery. It sometimes happens that one house finishes its business before the other. In such cases, a small number of members, usually those who represent nearby districts or states, meets from time to time, merely to fulfill this constitutional requirement. Although neither house may meet elsewhere in the United States, there is no constitutional barrier to individual members or committees conducting congressional business anywhere in the United States, or for that matter, anywhere in the world. It is common practice for congressional committees to hold hearings outside Washington, usually in the area then under investigation or study.

Section 6   Rights of Members

Clause 1. Compensation of Congressmen

> THE SENATORS AND REPRESENTATIVES SHALL RECEIVE A COMPENSATION FOR THEIR SERVICES, TO BE ASCERTAINED BY LAW, AND PAID OUT OF THE TREASURY OF THE UNITED STATES.

In recent years, Congress has been beset by the problem of agreeing on a system or formula that would authorize pay raises for themselves and other officials to keep pace with inflation while avoiding unfavorable criticism from the media and the public. Their latest try is an automatic cost of living adjustment (COLA) law passed in 1989 which provides for pay raises without a vote. Senators and Representatives in 1993 received the same compensation, $ 133,644, but this is being challenged by a number of congressmen as a violation of the new Twenty-Seventh Amendment.

In addition to an annual salary, congressmen receive other compensations and perquisites. They are given a yearly sum for clerical and administrative staffs and free space in a federal building for a home office. Postage, telephone, telegraph, and stationery allowances are also included in their congressional budget. A congressman has the "franking privilege" of sending official business through the mails for free. There are a number of other privileges such as free trips abroad while on government business (a junket), that add to the attractiveness of the position. A congressman is entitled to travel expenses to and from Washington and a favorable tax preferment for having to maintain residences in both Washington and the home district. In time, a member becomes eligible for a substantial pension.

Clause 1. [*continued*] IMMUNITIES OF MEMBERS

> THEY SHALL IN ALL CASES, EXCEPT TREASON, FELONY AND BREACH OF THE PEACE, BE PRIVILEGED FROM ARREST DURING THEIR ATTENDANCE AT THE SESSION OF THEIR RESPECTIVE HOUSES, AND IN GOING TO AND RETURNING FROM THE SAME; AND FOR ANY SPEECH OR DEBATE IN EITHER HOUSE, THEY SHALL NOT BE QUESTIONED IN ANY OTHER PLACE.

This clause protects congressmen from unwarranted interference with their legislative activities. The founding fathers, familiar with the Crown's intimidation of legislators in England and in the colonies, were determined that congressmen would be free from fear. Today, however, this provision is practically obsolete.

The privilege grants immunity from arrest only in civil suits, i.e., disputes between two citizens. It cannot protect a congressman from arrest in a case involving a crime, nor does it prevent a congressman from appearing in court as a witness, in either a criminal or civil suit. For example, a congressman could be arrested for bribery but could not be arrested for nonpayment of alimony. The part of the clause "except treason, felony, and breach of the peace," has been interpreted by the courts as withdrawing all criminal offenses from the scope of this privilege.

Members of the English Parliament were sometimes arrested and imprisoned by the kings for statements made in legislative chambers. To prevent intimidation of a free legislature, this clause prohibits anyone from punishing congressmen for what they say during the normal course of their proceedings. The protection also extends to statements made by members during committee hearings or otherwise engaged in the official business of the Congress. Finally, the privilege covers statements of witnesses testifying before congressional committees. Therefore a committee witness may unjustly accuse a person of being a criminal and that person could not do anything about it, except, perhaps, ask for an opportunity to deny the charge. On the other hand, if the same witness made the same accusation without benefit of congressional protection (say, in a newspaper interview), the accused could institute libel proceedings seeking judicial redress and possible monetary damages. In 1979 the Supreme Court narrowed the scope of legislative immunity by excluding certain non-legislative functions such as speeches, news releases, or newsletters.

Clause 2. Separation of Powers

> NO SENATOR OR REPRESENTATIVE SHALL, DURING THE TIME FOR WHICH HE WAS ELECTED, BE APPOINTED TO ANY CIVIL OFFICE UNDER THE AUTHORITY OF THE UNITED STATES, WHICH SHALL HAVE BEEN CREATED, OR THE EMOLUMENTS WHEREOF SHALL HAVE BEEN INCREASED DURING SUCH TIME; AND NO PERSON HOLDING ANY OFFICE UNDER THE UNITED STATES, SHALL BE A MEMBER OF EITHER HOUSE DURING HIS CONTINUANCE IN OFFICE.

The principle of *separation of powers* is reaffirmed in this clause. No congressman can be, at the same time, a member of the executive, judicial, or administrative branches of the government, except to serve as a temporary agent of the United States at international conferences. Furthermore, this clause prohibits a person from accepting a federal position which has either been created or had its salary increased while that person was a member of Congress. The reason behind this provision is to prevent a type of corruption whereby the legislature may promise a certain legislative action in return for the appointment of one of its members to a federal position. However, Congress may evade the literal meaning of the provision in order to make effective a legitimate appointment. For example, in 1907 Congress raised the salary of the Secretary of State. In 1909, it reduced the salary to its original figure, so that a member of the Senate at the time the increase was voted, would be eligible for the office of Secretary of State. History repeated itself in 1992 when Congress cut the salary of the Secretary of Treasury so that Senator Lloyd Bentsen could accept the appointment from President-elect Bill Clinton.

Section 7   Bills and Resolutions

Clause 1. Revenue Bills

> ALL BILLS FOR RAISING REVENUE SHALL ORIGINATE IN THE HOUSE OF REPRESENTATIVES; BUT THE SENATE MAY PROPOSE OR CONCUR WITH AMENDMENTS AS ON OTHER BILLS.

No taxation without representation! The old Revolutionary War battle cry was written into the Constitution in this clause. All bills for raising revenue (tax measure) *must* begin in the House of Representatives. The framers believed that elected Representatives would be closer to the people and more responsive to their wishes. Although the Seventeenth Amendment provides for the popular election of Senators, who also reflect public opinion, the constitutional provision remains as it was in 1787.

Although revenue bills start in the House, the Senate has the power to amend, alter, modify, or even substitute its own tax bill for that of the House. The two houses must agree on one bill before it may be submitted to the President for his signature. Therefore, whenever differences occur in bills passed by the two houses, a *conference* committee composed of members of both houses is appointed to negotiate such agreement. The delegations report back to their respective houses the results of these deliberations (usually a compromise) and a vote is taken on the conference committee's report.

Clause 2. <u>Veto of Bills</u>

EVERY BILL WHICH SHALL HAVE PASSED THE HOUSE OF REPRESENTATIVES AND THE SENATE, SHALL, BEFORE IT BECOME A LAW, BE PRESENTED TO THE PRESIDENT OF THE UNITED STATES; IF HE APPROVE HE SHALL SIGN IT, BUT IF NOT HE SHALL RETURN IT, WITH HIS OBJECTIONS TO THAT HOUSE IN WHICH IT SHALL HAVE ORIGINATED, WHO SHALL ENTER THE OBJECTIONS AT LARGE ON THEIR JOURNAL, AND PROCEED TO RECONSIDER IT, IF AFTER SUCH RECONSIDERATION TWO THIRDS OF THAT HOUSE SHALL AGREE TO PASS THE BILL, IT SHALL BE SENT, TOGETHER WITH THE OBJECTIONS, TO THE OTHER HOUSE, BY WHICH IT SHALL LIKEWISE BE RECONSIDERED, AND IF APPROVED BY TWO THIRDS OF THAT HOUSE, IT SHALL BECOME LAW, BUT IN ALL SUCH CASES THE VOTES OF BOTH HOUSES SHALL BE DETERMINED BY YEAS AND NAYS, AND THE NAMES OF THE PERSONS VOTING FOR AND AGAINST THE BILL SHALL BE ENTERED ON THE JOURNAL OF EACH HOUSE RESPECTIVELY, IF ANY BILL SHALL NOT BE RETURNED BY THE PERSIDENT WITHIN TEN DAYS (SUNDAYS EXCEPTED) AFTER IT SHALL HAVE BEEN PRESENTED TO HIM, THE SAME SHALL BE LAW IN LIKE MANNER AS IF HE HAD SIGNED IT, UNLESS THE CONGRESS BY THEIR ADJOURNMENT PREVENT ITS RETURN, IN WHICH CASE IT SHALL NOT BE A LAW.

This clause brings us to a consideration of another great principle of American government—the doctrine of *checks and balances*. Congress has the sole power of originating legislation, but a check is placed upon its legislative powers by this clause. The President is given what is often called a *qualified veto power*. That is, he may refuse to sign the bill. The President's veto power is balanced by the power of Congress to pass the bill over his veto by a two-thirds majority, thus permitting it to become law. Although this clause is included within the article on Congress, it actually deals with the President's veto powers.

When the President receives a bill that has been passed in identical form by both houses, he may choose one of four courses of action:

(1) If he approves of the bill, he may sign it and it becomes a part of U.S. law.

(2) If he does not approve of the bill, he may refuse to sign it and send it back to the house where it originated, stating his reasons for disapproval. This is often referred to as the *message veto*. If each house, acting separately, passes the bill again by a two-thirds vote, that is, two-thirds of a quorum, it becomes law without the President's signature. This action of the Congress is referred to as "a vote to override the veto." If the bill fails to gain the necessary two-thirds vote in either house, the veto is upheld and the measure does not become law.

(3) The President may keep the bill and if at the end of ten days (Sundays excepted) Congress is *still* in session, the bill becomes law without his signature. This provision was placed in the Constitution to prevent a President from defeating legislation by delay or inaction. Sometimes a President allows a bill to become law in this manner in order to show his displeasure, or because it may be politically unwise to veto the bill. For example, in 1943 Congress tacked on a "rider" (that is, something not pertinent to the subject of the bill) to an appropriation measure. This rider prohibited the Treasurer of the United States from paying salaries to three federal officials. President Franklin D. Roosevelt was opposed to the rider, yet funds were essential to the operation of government. Roosevelt allowed the entire bill to become law and showed his displeasure by refusing to sign it.

Some state governors could have handled the situation in a simpler fashion because they have what is called the *item veto*. They can approve parts of bills while disapproving other parts. The President cannot do this. He has to approve of the entire bill or disapprove of it as a whole.

(4) The President may keep the bill, though refusing to sign it. If at the end of ten days (Sundays excluded) Congress has adjourned, the bill does not become law. This action of the President is referred to as the *pocket veto.* This is the most absolute or final of the President's veto powers because Congress cannot do anything about it except to introduce the same bill in the next session.

One may ask, "Why would a President choose to follow this course of action?" Usually partisan politics is at the core of the matter. The bill might have much support in Congress, and in the general public. If he vetoes it with a message, his veto may be overridden, and he suffers a political defeat. At any rate, a debate in Congress would stir up considerable sentiment. If he can quietly kill the bill with a pocket veto, so much the better, for him. Congress, of course, knows of this practice and sometimes forestalls the pocket veto by staying in session until the President has had time to review the bills sent to him. Federal courts agreed with Senator Edward M. Kennedy's interpretation that the pocket veto pertained only to final adjournment and not to situations of Congress taking a brief recess or adjourning between sessions.

Clause 3. <u>Presidential Approval of Legislation</u>

> EVERY ORDER, RESOLUTION, OR VETO TO WHICH THE CONCURRENCE OF THE SENATE AND HOUSE OF REPRESENTATIVES MAY BE NECESSARY (EXCEPT ON A QUESTION OF ADJOURNMENT) SHALL BE PRESENTED TO THE PRESIDENT OF THE UNITED STATES; AND BEFORE THE SAME SHALL TAKE EFFECT, SHALL BE APPROVED BY HIM, OR BEING DISAPPROVED BY HIM, SHALL BE REPASSED BY TWO THIRDS OF THE SENATE AND HOUSE OF REPRESENTATIVES, ACCORDING TO THE RULES AND LIMITATIONS PRESCRIBED IN THE CASE OF A BILL.

Congress would, if required to abide by the literal meaning of this clause, bog down in legislative stagnation. In practice, not every order, resolution, or vote requires a presidential signature, or lacking that, a two-thirds vote. Custom, tradition, and practical necessity have forced Congress to adopt a more liberal view.

Proposed constitutional amendments are not submitted to the President because Congress is acting under its constituent powers delegated by Article 5 of the Constitution. *Concurrent resolutions,* which do not become law, are also exempt from executive review. *Simple resolutions* or *orders* expressing the opinions of the Congress or of one house are likewise free of presidential influence. *Public bills, private bills,* and *joint resolutions* require presidential approval.

Although used sparingly, the so-called congressional veto came into extensive use after the President Nixon-Congress confrontations of the early 1970s. The "veto" is a legislative device to check presidential power or to override an executive action of which the Congress disapproves. Simply stated, Congress, or even one House, may nullify or countermand a specific presidential action by means of a concurrent resolution or by including a nullifying clause in a law delegating power to the executive. A good example is the War Powers Resolution of 1973, passed over President Nixon's veto, that required the President to report to Congress on overseas troop commitments. This law allowed Congress, at any time U.S. forces were engaged in hostilities without a declaration of war or specific congressional authorization, by concurrent resolution to direct the President to disengage such troops. The executive branch felt that the "congressional veto," especially those resolutions that permit one House to negate presidential action, was an unconstitutional encroachment upon the separation of power. The Supreme Court agreed in 1983, whereupon Congress instituted other means to gain control over the executive branch.

Section 8   Powers of Congress

The sections discussed thus far have dealt with the internal operations of the Congress. This section, one of the most important in our Constitution, is concerned with the powers of Congress. Here is striking evidence that our framers believed in a limited government—a government of *enumerated powers.* Beginning with Clause 1 we will take up seventeen separate and distinct powers which the framers conferred on Congress. An eighteenth power, the so-called *necessary and proper* clause was added to aid Congress in carrying out the other *expressed powers.*

By combining an expressed power with the "necessary and proper" clause, we have what is often called an *implied power* of Congress. Thus the power to coin money and regulate its value (Clause 5) plus the "necessary and proper" clause gives Congress the implied power to incorporate a Bank of the United States (a power which is not specifically conferred on Congress).

From a combination of several expressed powers, usually with the "necessary and proper" clause, we have what is commonly called a *resulting* power. Thus the powers to wage war (Clause 11), to make treaties (Article III), to govern the District of Columbia (Clause 17), and to make rules and regulations for territories (Article IV) give the national government power to acquire territory.

These distinctions among expressed, implied, and resulting powers are essential for understanding the great range of powers possessed by Congress. It will also be useful to know the difference between *exclusive powers* and *concurrent powers.* An exclusive power is one that is possessed entirely and completely by the national government. For example, only Congress can declare war (Clause 11). A concurrent power is one that both the national government and the states can exercise at the same time over the same subjects. For example, both the national government and the states levy taxes upon the same individual.

Clause 1. <u>Power to Tax</u>

> THE CONGRESS SHALL HAVE POWER TO LAY AND COLLECT TAXES, DUTIES, IMPOSTS AND EXCISES, TO PAY THE DEBTS AND PROVIDE FOR THE COMMON DEFENCE AND GENERAL WELFARE OF THE UNITED STATES; BUT ALL DUTIES, IMPOSTS AND EXCISES SHALL BE UNIFORM THROUGHOUT THE UNITED STATES.

Significantly the very first power given to Congress is the power to tax, a most necessary power for any government. Not only has

Congress the power to levy taxes, but it also has the power to use various means to collect the taxes (withholding money from your paycheck, for example). Congress can tax and spend the money for purposes other than those definitely listed in this section. For example, the Constitution does not mention such activities as housing, conservation, or education, yet each year Congress appropriates millions of dollars to aid these activities.

Congress not only can aid, but it also can regulate individuals and businesses by means of its taxing powers. It may make the rate of taxation on the privilege of receiving an inheritance so high as to hinder the accumulation of wealth. Or it may discourage or cripple an evil activity through high taxes. For example, gambling, particularly where it is tied in with the nationwide crime syndicates, is looked upon as an evil. So in 1951 Congress passed a law that required operators of handbooks ("bookies") to obtain a federal tax stamp (and also to submit their names and places of business). In addition, the law required these operators to pay a tax of 10 percent upon their gross earnings. Failure to register and pay taxes would result in federal prosecution. Congress didn't expect to obtain large revenues from this act. In fact, it would be pleased if the tax returned no revenue. The main purpose of the law was to make the operation of handbooks difficult. Enforced for over a decade, a challenge to the law's constitutionality was upheld by the Court in 1968. If the gamblers complied with registration, state and local governments could obtain their names and addresses, raid their locations, and prosecute. There are a number of other examples whereby the national government has used its taxing powers to protect the safety, health, welfare, and morals of the people of the United States. This action on the part of the government is sometimes called the *national police powers.*

Uniformity means geographic conformity. The same tax will fall with the same force or effect upon the same article wherever it may be found in the United States. Different articles may be taxed at different rates, but, for example, if liquor is taxed at $1.00 a gallon in Chicago, it has to be taxed $1.00 in New York, New Orleans, or wherever it is manufactured.

Clause 2. <u>Power to Borrow Money</u>

The Congress shall have power ...

TO BORROW MONEY ON THE CREDIT OF THE UNITED STATES.

Congress borrows money by selling government securities—bonds, treasury notes, or treasury certificates. Anybody may buy these securities. The government is under obligation to redeem them at some future date, stated on the security; meanwhile it pays interest during the life of the indebtedness.

Clause 3. <u>Power to Regulate Commerce</u>

The Congress shall have power ...

TO REGULATE COMMERCE WITH FOREIGN NATIONS; AND AMONG THE SEVERAL STATES; AND WITH INDIAN TRIBES.

When we discussed the weaknesses in the Articles of Confederation, we noted that one of the main defects was the erection of trade barriers among states. The framers were so concerned about this problem that they gave Congress exclusive control over commercial relations with foreign countries (foreign commerce) and over the commerce among the states (interstate commerce). The commerce with Indian tribes is of minor significance today.

But what is commerce? Narrowly, the dictionary defines commerce as the "exchange or buying or selling of commodities on a large scale between different places." Very early in our history Chief Justice John Marshall gave a much broader meaning to the term in the famous case of *Gibbons v. Ogden* (1824). Commerce meant much more than trade or buying and selling. To Marshall it meant commercial intercourse, which included navigation. Marshall's interpretation was expanded to cover the movement of practically anything or everything across state lines. Congress's power extended not only to the things themselves (individuals, commodities, livestock) but also to their method of movement (railroads, airplanes, trucks, ships, buses, telephone, telegraph, radio, and television). Thus a person walking over a bridge between Illinois and Iowa would be as much a part of interstate commerce as the transportation of a new automobile from Detroit to Los Angeles.

In the early decades of our history, Congress and the federal courts were concerned with preventing states from interfering with the free flow of interstate commerce. Thus if a state law required an interstate train to stop at every city on its route, the courts would rule the law null and void. Even if the commerce were entirely within the jurisdiction of the states (intrastate commerce), Congress's powers would be superior if the state law substantially affected interstate commerce. For example, a tax levied by Montana upon each telephone instrument in use in that state was held invalid, because it placed an excessive burden on that interstate business. On the basis of congressional power to regulate commerce, the Supreme Court has upheld various civil rights acts banning discrimination in places of public accommodation such as hotels, resorts, and restaurants.

Subsidy payments to airlines and shippers help to regulate our commerce. Also the power to regulate means the power to bar from the channels of interstate commerce certain undesirable items. Lottery tickets cannot be transported in interstate commerce (protection of morals); impure and misbranded foods and drugs are banned (protection of health); and railroad cars not having air brakes are excluded (protection of safety). Numerous other examples can be cited of the exercise of the national government's police power through the commerce clause.

It is apparent that the power to regulate interstate and foreign commerce is a tremendously important and far-reaching power. It has fostered the development of an industrial and business system unsurpassed in the world today. As Chief Justice Marshall once said, "for all commercial purposes we are one nation."

Clause 4. Naturalization

The Congress shall have the power ...

TO ESTABLISH AN UNIFORM RULE OF NATURALIZATION, AND ...

Naturalization is the process whereby an alien (a person owing allegiance to another country) becomes a citizen by some official act. In the words of the Supreme Court, naturalization is "an act of adopting a foreigner, and clothing him with the privileges of a native-born citizen."

Congress has complete control over which foreigners may become citizens of the United States, and has established a very elaborate procedure that aliens must follow. Naturalization may be *collective* or *individual.* Collective naturalization occurs when Congress, by law, extends citizenship to large groups of people. For example, in 1976 Congress granted U.S. citizenship to all Northern Mariana Islands. Individual naturalization is the more common method of acquiring citizenship.

An alien may apply to either a federal court or a state court for a petition of naturalization. He fills out the papers ("first papers"); the Immigration and Naturalization Service checks his background and personal traits and examines him on his knowledge of American principles; he makes a declaration to become a citizen ("second papers"); and finally he is examined by a judge. If he passes these screenings and tests, he takes an oath of allegiance and receives his certificate of naturalization ("third papers").

Under the current regulations practically every alien has an opportunity to become a citizen. Minimum requirements include: five years lawful, permanent residence in the United States (physically present at least half the time); eighteen years of age; ability to read, write, and speak ordinary English; good moral character; belief in and knowledge of U.S. government, institutions, history, and principles; and oath of allegiance to the United States and renunciation of allegiance to his or her former country. Some exceptions to these general requirements exist for special classes of aliens.

At one time our naturalization laws barred practically all Asians from ever becoming citizens even though their children, if born in the United States, were citizens (see Amendment 14, Section 1). Today, no such general ban applies to any race, nationality, or section of the world. However, a person cannot become a citizen who, at any time during a ten-year period before he or she files the petition for naturalization, advocated, belonged to, or supported organizations (such as the Communist party) which believe in the violent overthrow of government.

Since citizenship is a privilege granted by the government, it may be taken away by either *expatriation* or *denaturalization.* Expatriation is a voluntary renunciation of citizenship, and therefore applies to both native born and naturalized citizens. The law lists a number of activities in addition to a formal renunciation that result in loss of citizenship—including becoming a naturalized citizen of a foreign country, accepting a job in a foreign government, taking an oath of allegiance to a foreign country, deserting in time of war, and committing treason. Constitutional scholars indicate these presumptions of expatriation are of dubious validity. A naturalized citizen no longer loses his citizenship by reason of expatriation if he resides in any foreign nation, including his own foreign country.

Denaturalization may be ordered by a federal court in the event that the government proves that citizenship was obtained by illegal or fraudulent means. For example, if an alien knowingly hides the fact that he was a member of a subversive organization at the time of his naturalization and later the government can prove this willful fraud, then the court could take away that person's citizenship. During the 1970s, federal courts denaturalized several former members of the Hitler Nazi party because they had given fraudulent information on their naturalization petitions. Denaturalization therefore applies only to naturalized citizens and not to native-born citizens.

Clause 4. [continued] Bankruptcy

The Congress shall have the power to establish ...

UNIFORM LAWS ON THE SUBJECT OF BANKRUPTCIES THROUGHOUT THE UNITED STATES;

A bankrupt is a person whose total debts exceed his ability to repay them. Congress has provided a way in which the debtor may discharge his obligations to his creditors. The law aids creditors by distributing the debtor's assets among them, instead of paying one creditor in full perhaps and the others nothing. A person who goes through bankruptcy proceedings can start anew without having a heavy burden hanging over his head.

Clause 5. Power Over Monetary Systems

The Congress shall have power ...

TO COIN MONEY, REGULATE THE VALUE THEREOF, AND OF FOREIGN COIN, AND FIX THE STANDARD OF WEIGHTS AND MEASURES;

This clause gives Congress the authority to regulate practically every phase of our monetary system. Congress may incorporate banks, establish a Federal Reserve System, and make paper money acceptable payment of all debts. Acting under the authority of this clause, Congress, in 1933, required all persons to exchange their gold coin and gold certificates for a currency that could not be converted into gold again. Congress permitted ownership and sale of gold again in 1974.

Clause 6. Preventing Counterfeiting

The Congress shall have the power ...

TO PROVIDE FOR THE PUNISHMENT OF COUNTERFEITING THE SECURITIES AND CURRENT COIN OF THE UNITED STATES;

The stability of any government rests on the soundness of its currency. Therefore Congress must possess power to protect its coin and currency from being counterfeited. For this reason, Congress also has enacted laws establishing penalties for counterfeiting within the United States the coin or currencies of foreign countries.

Clause 7. Establishing Post Offices and Roads

The Congress shall have the power ...

TO ESTABLISH POST OFFICES AND POST ROADS;

This power is not confined to merely designating this place as a post office and that road as a post road. It gives Congress the positive power to construct post offices and roads and to maintain them. Moreover, it gives Congress the necessary authority to punish anyone interfering with the speedy and safe delivery of the mails. The postal power gives Congress authority to exclude from the mails any publication designed to defraud or corrupt the morals of the public. For example, a lewd and vulgar magazine may not be sent through the mails.

The postal power, combined with other powers, especially the commerce power, gives Congress authority to appropriate money, in the form of subsidies for carrying the mail, to railroads, shipping companies, and airlines. Also, these same powers permit Congress to make grants-in-aid to states for the purpose of constructing and maintaining roads and highways.

Clause 8. <u>Power over Patents and Copyrights</u>

The Congress shall have power ...

TO PROMOTE THE PROCESS OF SCIENCE AND USEFUL ARTS, BY SECURING FOR LIMITED TIMES TO AUTHORS AND INVENTORS THE EXCLUSIVE RIGHT TO THEIR RESPECTIVE WRITINGS AND DISCOVERIES;

This clause provides the basis for our national *copyright* and patent laws. Notice, however, that neither of these terms appears in the above clause. A copyright is an exclusive right to reproduce, publish, or sell an original composition or work of art. It protects artists, musicians, and authors by giving them exclusive control over their paintings, musical compositions, books, articles, maps, photographs, and the like. In 1978, Congress, in the first major revision in seventy years, granted these exclusive rights for a period consisting of the life of the author and fifty years after the author's death. At the end of this time, exclusive rights terminate and the work of art becomes a part of the public domain, subject to use and reproduction by anyone. Special rules apply to anonymous, pseudonyms, joint, and works made for hire.

A patent is a similar exclusive right given to inventors for the protection of their discoveries. However, in order to secure a patent, the device must be new and must be *useful*. Mere gadgets—a clay doorknob instead of wood or metal—are not patentable. A patent runs for seventeen years and is not renewable.

Copyrights and patents are considered a form of property and may be sold, leased, willed, or even inherited. Controversies involving patents may be taken to a special court, the United States Court of Custom and Patent Appeals. *Trademarks* are not protected by this clause, although Congress has provided for them under its interstate commerce clause.

Obtaining a copyright is a simple matter—deposit two copies of the work and pay a small fee to the Copyright Office in the Library of Congress. A copyright will be issued if the work of art is original. Patents are more difficult to obtain since proof of the invention's originality and usefulness must first be determined. The Patent and Trademark Office is in the Department of Commerce.

Clause 9. Establish Inferior Courts

The Congress shall have power ...

TO CONSTITUTE TRIBUNALS INFERIOR TO THE SUPREME COURT;

The Supreme Court is the only court mentioned by name in the Constitution. All other federal courts have been established by Congress. In Article III, Section I, Congress is again given the power to create inferior courts. This clause provides the basis of the so-called legislative courts described in Article III.

Clause 10. Piracy and Felonies on the High Seas

The Congress shall have power ...

TO DEFINE AND PUNISH PIRACIES AND FELONIES COMMITTED ON THE HIGH SEAS, AND OFFENCES AGAINST THE LAW OF NATIONS;

This clause gives Congress the power to prescribe punishments for any offense committed on a U.S. vessel. This applies to a vessel either in the middle of the ocean or lying at anchor within the territorial waters of another country. Congress also has the power to make any crime under the law of nations (international law) a crime under the laws of the United States. Congress is under no obligation to do this, but President Jimmy Carter's emphasis on world human rights and the agreement respecting individual rights signed at Helsinki, Finland, in 1975 by most of the major countries could make this clause very important in future years.

Clause 11. Declare War

The Congress shall have power ...

> TO DECLARE WAR, GRANT LETTERS OF MARQUE AND REPRISAL, AND MAKE RULES CONCERNING CAPTURES ON LAND AND WATER;

Clause 12. Maintain Armed Services

The Congress shall have power ...

> TO RAISE AND SUPPORT ARMIES, BUT NO APPROPRIATION OF MONEY TO THAT USE SHALL BE FOR A LONGER TERM THAN TWO YEARS;

Clause 13. Establish a Navy

The Congress shall have power ...

> TO PROVIDE AND MAINTAIN A NAVY;

Clause 14. Control Armed Services

The Congress shall have power ...

> TO MAKE RULES FOR THE GOVERNMENT AND REGULATION OF THE LAND AND NAVAL FORCES;

These are the so-called *war powers* of Congress. Congress alone has the power to transform the United States from a state of peace to a state of war. That is, Congress authorizes the United States *to go to war*. If, however, the United States is attacked and the President orders our forces to resist, a declaration of war is unnecessary, since we would already be *at war*. The power to declare war also means the power to *conduct* and *wage* war.

The founding fathers believed that this very important power that affects the lives of all the people should not be given to one person. Therefore they placed it with the Congress, as representatives of the people. It is true, however, that a President may use his powers as commander-in-chief of the armed forces in such a manner as to leave Congress no choice but to declare war. President James Polk, for example, forced Congress's hand, and the Mexican War resulted in 1848. Actions of recent Presidents with respect to hostilities in Korea and Vietnam, where no formal declaration of war was made by Congress, have raised serious constitutional questions. However, the Supreme Court has avoided making a definitive decision.

Letters of marque and reprisal are only of historical interest today. They were authorizations to individuals to conduct *private* warfare upon the ships of an enemy. The official sanction then exempted them from being considered pirates.

Perhaps a specific constitutional grant of power to raise and maintain armies and navies is not absolutely needed. The principle that the framers were emphasizing was that *Congress* was the branch of government that controlled the armed services (the Air Force today is included in the meaning of army).

The framers, drawing upon their colonial experience, considered a permanent or *standing army* a threat to the liberties of the people. Therefore they restricted appropriations for the support of the army to a two-year period. This would force army leaders to come to Congress periodically and thus prevent a buildup of armed might without congressional consent. The navy was not to be so feared; therefore no qualifying conditions were placed on its appropriations. Under its powers to prescribe rules and regulations, Congress has established a system of justice for military personnel that lies outside the regular judicial process. Such protections as indictment by grand jury or double jeopardy do not apply to servicemen. Furthermore, the decisions of a court-martial, acting within the scope of its jurisdiction, are not controlled or reviewed by the civil courts, but may be appealed to the United States Court of Military Appeals made up of three civilian judges appointed by the President and confirmed by the Senate for fifteen year terms. The Supreme Court has limited Congress's power to govern military personnel by explicitly excluding civilian employees and civilian dependents from military justice. Nor can the military jurisdiction extend to any person who was not a member of the armed forces at the time of the offense and trial. Therefore, a discharged soldier cannot be tried by the military for any offense committed while in the service.

It would be a mistake to think that Congress's war powers concern only the military establishment. In contemporary society, war is total war involving the entire population. Under such circumstances Congress's power is tremendous. The wide scope of authority exercised by Congress under the war powers is illustrated by such actions as: the drafting of men into the armed services, the confiscation and distribution of vital war materials to manufacturers, the enactment of price and rent controls, the regulation of the use of raw materials and food consumption, and even the seizing and operating of manufacturing plants closed by strikes. In short, under modern conditions of warfare, the Congress and the President have what amounts to complete control over the industrial and human resources of the nation.

Clause 15. Control Over the Militia

The Congress shall have power ...

TO PROVIDE FOR CALLING FORTH THE MILITIA TO EXECUTE THE LAWS OF THE UNION, SUPPRESS INSURRECTIONS AND REPEL INVASIONS;

Clause 16. Control Over the Militia

The Congress shall have power ...

TO PROVIDE FOR ORGANIZING, ARMING, AND DISCIPLINING THE MILITIA, AND FOR GOVERNING SUCH PART OF THEM AS MAY BE EMPLOYED IN THE SERVICE OF THE UNITED STATES, RESERVING TO THE STATES RESPECTIVELY, THE APPOINTMENT OF THE OFFICERS, AND THE AUTHORITY OF TRAINING THE MILITIA ACCORDING TO THE DISCIPLINE PRESCRIBED BY CONGRESS;

Today the militia is known as the *National Guard.* In 1795 Congress delegated to the President the power to call out the militia. In the course of history he has used this power in a number of instances. He can, of course, use the regular U.S. forces to suppress insurrections and would certainly do so in the case of invasion.

Notice that Congress and the states share in the supervision of the National Guard. Ultimate control rests with the national government. Congress supplies most of the funds and establishes the general rules for training, disciplining, and otherwise governing the personnel. The states, usually the governors, appoint the officers and supervise the actual training. The state governments may use their militia to quell riots, police disaster areas, or even fight forest fires. The national government may call the militia into federal service— which was done during the segregation controversies in Arkansas and Mississippi. In such cases, the National Guard became a part of the U.S. armed forces. As military units and as individuals, the Guard comes directly under the control of Congress and the President. In the Little Rock, Arkansas, case, President Dwight D. Eisenhower "federalized" the Arkansas National Guard, thus bringing it directly under the jurisdiction of the federal government. This action was taken over the strong objections of the Arkansas governor, but the President's power was upheld. President John F. Kennedy, over the Mississippi governor's opposition, federalized that state's Guard in 1962 during the University of Mississippi crisis.

Clause 17. Govern Territories

The Congress shall have the power ...

TO EXERCISE EXCLUSIVE LEGISLATION IN ALL CASES

WHATSOEVER, OVER SUCH DISTRICT (NOT EXCEEDING TEN MILES SQUARE) AS MAY, BY CESSION OF PARTICULAR STATES, AND THE ACCEPTANCE OF CONGRESS, BECOME THE SEAT OF THE GOVERNMENT OF THE UNITED STATES, AND TO EXERCISE LIKE AUTHORITY OVER ALL PLACES PURCHASED BY THE CONSENT OF THE LEGISLATURE OF THE STATE IN WHICH THE SAME SHALL BE, FOR THE ERECTION OF FORTS, MAGAZINES, ARSENALS, DOCKYARDS, AND OTHER NEEDFUL BUILDINGS;

Congress created the District of Columbia, including the city of Washington. The citizens of the District are citizens of the United States, but not of any state. The present form of the government for the District dates from 1975 when a home rule charter went into effect. Congress retained a broad veto and significant fiscal powers, but the day-to-day legislative and administrative functions are carried out by an elected Mayor and a thirteen-member council, eight elected by wards and five, at large. The Mayor and council have the usual powers over personnel, budget, ordinances, etc., but as sort of a tradeoff for Congress's ultimate control, the federal government contributes about a third of the District's annual income. Since 1970, District voters elect one delegate to the House of Representatives. This person can speak and vote in committee sessions, but can only speak (not vote) on the floor of the House. Rule changes in 1993 allow the District Representative (also other territorial representatives) to vote in the Committee of the Whole House, but such votes would not count if they were significant in the passage or failure of a particular bill. The Twenty-Third Amendment now gives citizens of the District the right to vote for presidential and vice-presidential candidates. Three electoral votes are allocated to the District of Columbia. Another amendment proposed in 1978 would repeal the Twenty-Third Amendment and make the District equal to the states in the matter of representation in Congress, presidential voting, electoral college, and ratifying constitutional amendments.

Congress may purchase land from the states for purposes other than those listed in this clause.

Clause 18. Necessary and Proper Clause

The Congress shall have power ...

> TO MAKE ALL LAWS WHICH SHALL BE NECESSARY AND
> PROPER FOR CARRYING INTO EXECUTION THE FOREGOING POWERS,
> AND ALL OTHER POWERS VESTED BY THIS CONSTITUTION IN THE
> GOVERNMENT OF THE UNITED STATES, OR IN ANY DEPARTMENT
> OR OFFICE THEREOF.

This clause is often referred to as the *necessary and proper clause* or the *elastic clause.* This clause does not give Congress the power to enact laws on any subject it so desires. Neither does this clause restrict Congress to the enactment of laws that are indispensable. What this clause does is to give Congress the means whereby it may effectively execute its enumerated powers and those of the other branches of government.

There is no doubt that this clause expands Congress's authority. A study of constitutional law shows that almost every power possessed by the federal government has been expanded in some degree by the use of the elastic clause. The use to which this clause is put can be best illustrated by several examples:

There is no specific grant of power to Congress in the Constitution to incorporate a national bank. Yet, the court decided a bank was an appropriate means for levying and collecting taxes and regulating commerce. Likewise, the chartering of a railroad company was a necessary means for promoting commerce and waging war.

The powers to tax, borrow money, pay debts, and coin money, together with the elastic clause, give Congress almost complete control over the monetary system of the United States.

Section 9   Prohibitions on Congress

Clause 1. Importation of Slaves

> THE MIGRATION OR IMPORTATION OF SUCH PERSONS AS ANY
> OF THE STATES NOW EXISTING SHALL THINK PROPER TO ADMIT,
> SHALL NOT BE PROHIBITED BY THE CONGRESS PRIOR TO THE YEAR

ONE THOUSAND EIGHT HUNDRED AND EIGHT, BUT A TAX OR DUTY
MAY BE IMPOSED ON SUCH IMPORTATION, NOT EXCEEDING TEN
DOLLARS FOR EACH PERSON.

This clause refers to a future ban on the importation of slaves
into the United States. The ban went into effect twenty years after the
adoption of the Constitution, in 1808 to be exact. The Civil War
Amendments made this clause obsolete.

Clause 2. Suspension of Writ of *Habeas Corpus*

THE PRIVILEGE OF THE WRIT OF HABEAS CORPUS SHALL NOT
BE SUSPENDED, UNLESS WHEN IN CASES OF REBELLION OR INVASION
THE PUBLIC SAFETY MAY REQUIRE IT.

The writ of *habeas corpus* is one of the foremost protections of
our personal liberty. It is held in such high esteem that only rebellion
or invasion may provoke its suspension within the United States.
Writ of *habeas corpus* is a court order to a person who is detaining
another, requiring the jailer to bring the accused before the court and
show why he is being detained. If the judge believes that there are
insufficient reasons for holding the accused in custody, he may order
his release. Thus we see that this writ is used to obtain the liberation
of persons who are imprisoned without just cause.

Federal judges may issue the writ on federal and state officials,
but state judges are confined to their own state authorities. Congress,
by law, allowed federal courts to review convictions brought to their
attention from any court, to see if the legal processes had been correct.

The writ may be suspended during grave emergencies. But who
has the authority to order its suspension was a cause of concern for
many years. At the outbreak of the Civil War President Abraham
Lincoln authorized the military to suspend the writ in certain areas.
Some persons, particularly Chief Justice Roger Taney of the Supreme
Court, questioned his authority. At the close of the war, the Supreme
Court implied that only Congress had such power since the writ was
mentioned in Article I, Section 9, which deals with Congress and not

the presidency. The Congress, however, may delegate to the President the authority to suspend the writ under specific conditions.

Clause 3. Bills of Attainder and Ex Post Facto Laws

NO BILL OF ATTAINDER OR EX POST FACTOR LAW SHALL BE PASSED.

A bill of attainder is something mentioned infrequently in this century. The idea came into our Constitution as a result of certain practices in England in the seventeenth and eighteenth centuries, practices which our forebears wanted to prohibit in the United States. A bill of attainder is a legislative act that inflicts punishment without a judicial trial. Congress passed a law that forbade the President to pay the salaries of three officials unless he submitted their names for Senate approval. The Supreme Court, in 1946, declared this law unconstitutional as being a bill of attainder because it imposed a punishment (loss of pay) without a trial.

An *ex post facto* law is another type of law that had its origin in our early troubles with the British authorities. An *ex post facto* law is simply a retroactive (having effect in a prior time) criminal law that acts to the disadvantage of the accused. For example, Jones does something today and it is not a crime. Tomorrow Congress makes such action a crime and the national government tries to convict Jones for his original action. Such a law as applied to Jones would be declared *ex post facto,* and therefore unconstitutional. Or if Smith were arrested for mail fraud today when the penalty, on conviction is five years, but Congress should increase it to ten years, Smith could not be sentenced for the longer term because of this constitutional provision. Note that we have said that *ex post facto* laws are retroactive *criminal laws.* A retroactive civil law is perfectly legal. That is, in July Congress could pass a new tax law making it applicable to the first of January. The law has to act to the disadvantage of the accused. If Congress reduced the penalty, in the earlier example from five to three years, this would not be *ex post facto.*

Clause 4. Direct Taxes

> NO CAPITATION, OR OTHER DIRECT, TAX SHALL BE LAID,
> UNLESS IN PROPORTION TO THE CENSUS OR ENUMERATION HEREIN
> BEFORE DIRECTED TO BE TAKEN.

A capitation tax is a uniform tax imposed on each head or person—in other words, a poll tax. "Other direct taxes" are difficult to define, but usually taxes on land, and of course on income, are included. This constitutional requirement was inserted into the Constitution to eliminate the fears of southern states that their Negroes would be subject to a specific tax. (*See Amendment XVI*)

Clause 5. Export Taxes

> NO TAX OR DUTY SHALL BE LAID ON ARTICLES EXPORTED
> FROM ANY STATE.

Congress cannot tax as an export an article exported from a state. It may, however, levy a general tax that may hit an article intended for export purposes only. Also, Congress may prohibit exports to foreign countries under its commerce power. President Thomas Jefferson, for example, placed an embargo on U.S. goods intended for Great Britain and France during the Napoleonic Wars, and President Reagan likewise embargoed high-technology exports to Libya and imports of oil from Libya in 1982.

Clause 6. Preferential Treatment To Ports

> NO PREFERENCE SHALL BE GIVEN BY ANY REGULATION OF
> COMMERCE OR REVENUE TO THE PORTS OF ONE STATE OVER THOSE
> OF ANOTHER: NOR SHALL VESSELS BOUND TO, OR FROM, ONE
> STATE, BE OBLIGED TO ENTER, CLEAR OR PAY DUTIES IN ANOTHER.

This clause is intended to prevent Congress from giving preference to the ports of one state over those of another state. It does not interfere with Congress's powers to establish ports of entry, build lighthouses, or dredge channels in the individual ports of the United States.

Clause 7. Appropriations and Claims

> NO MONEY SHALL BE DRAWN FROM THE TREASURY, BUT IN CONSEQUENCE OF APPROPRIATIONS MADE BY LAW; AND A REGULAR STATEMENT AND ACCOUNT OF THE RECEIPTS AND EXPENDITURES OF ALL PUBLIC MONEY SHALL BE PUBLISHED FROM TIME TO TIME.

No claim against the United States for money may be honored unless Congress has provided for its appropriation by law. Thus, Congress has control of the purse strings, and it is well known that whoever pays the piper calls the tunes.

Clause 8. Titles of Nobility and Awards

> NO TITLE OF NOBILITY SHALL BE GRANTED BY THE UNITED STATES: AND NO PERSON HOLDING ANY OFFICE OF PROFIT OR TRUST UNDER THEM, SHALL, WITHOUT THE CONSENT OF THE CONGRESS, ACCEPT OF ANY PRESENT, EMOLUMENT, OFFICE, OR TITLE, OF ANY KIND WHATEVER, FROM ANY KING, PRINCE, OR FOREIGN STATE,

This clause was put into the Constitution to prevent foreign governments undermining our government through bribes, honors, or awards to our public officials. However, Congress may allow exceptions, e.g., it permitted General Eisenhower to receive the Order of Lenin from the Russian government. In 1967, it passed a law allowing officials to accept and keep gifts from foreign sources that are of "minimal value" (under $100). Gifts over that amount are accepted on behalf of the U.S. government and turned over to the General Services Administrator for use or later disposal.

Section 10   Prohibitions On the States

Clause 1. Treaties, Bills of Credit, Bills of Attainder, Obligation of Contract

> NO STATE SHALL ENTER INTO ANY TREATY, ALLIANCE, OR

CONFEDERATION; GRANT LETTERS OF MARQUE AND REPRISAL; COIN
MONEY; EMIT BILLS OF CREDIT; MAKE ANY THING BUT GOLD AND
SILVER COIN A TENDER IN PAYMENT OF DEBTS; PASS ANY BILL OF
ATTAINDER, EX POST FACTO LAW, OR LAW IMPAIRING THE
OBLIGATION OF CONTRACTS, OR GRANT ANY TITLE OF NOBILITY.

The national government has *complete* power with respect to our relations with foreign nations. The states have no power whatsoever to negotiate treaties or enter into any type of alliance with foreign countries.

The section on *letters of marque and reprisal* is obsolete under twentieth century methods of waging war. In the eighteenth and early nineteenth century it was quite common for nations to permit private individuals to outfit ships to harass and capture enemy vessels. Thus these letters were permits to privateers, and by this clause the states were prohibited from issuing them.

The states cannot coin or mint money, nor can they make paper money a medium of exchange between individuals or between individuals and the government. This is what is meant by "emitting bills of credit." Its inclusion in this section stems from the chaotic period after the Revolution when many state legislatures passed laws making paper money acceptable for payment of all debts. Then these legislatures proceeded to authorize issue after issue of paper money, which had the effect of reducing the value of their money. The debtors, of course, favored this type of policy, but creditors opposed it strenuously and were successful in securing the acceptance of this clause at the Constitutional Convention.

Bills of attainder and *ex post facto* laws have been discussed in Article I, Section 8, Clause 3. This clause prohibits states from passing such acts. Likewise, granting titles of nobility is banned—instead, Kentucky colonels and Oklahoma admirals are common.

"No state shall pass any law impairing the obligations of contracts." This sentence provided the basis of considerable court litigation until the middle of the nineteenth century. It was used by a great many persons and corporations as a means of protecting their property from what they considered unwarranted interference by the states. At first it was invoked against state laws which, for example, prevented the collection of a valid debt. Later on, it was used to protect certain franchises or special privileges which corporations had received from state legislatures, privileges legislatures later sought to take away or restrict. An actual case will illustrate the point. Dartmouth College had received a charter from the colonial legislature in 1769. This was reaffirmed by the new state legislature. In 1816 the state legislature sought to change Dartmouth from a private college to a state institution. The trustees of Dartmouth objected and took their case to the U.S. Supreme Court. The Court held that the charter given to Dartmouth was a contract which future legislatures could not change without the consent of the college.

After the 1840s the courts began to whittle down the broad meaning of this contract clause, realizing that the states must have some power to deal with corporations they had created. Gradually the courts took the position that any contract included within it, by implication, the existing law of the state. In this manner the states were not bargaining away their rights and duties to protect their citizens. After 1900 the contract clause, as it is often called, was superseded by the due process of law clause of the Fourteenth Amendment as the basic protection of property rights.

Clause 2. Imports and Export Taxes

NO STATE SHALL, WITHOUT THE CONSENT OF THE CONGRESS, LAY ANY IMPOSTS OR DUTIES ON IMPORTS OR EXPORTS, EXCEPT WHAT MAY BE ABSOLUTELY NECESSARY FOR EXECUTING ITS INSPECTION LAWS: AND THE NET PRODUCE OF ALL DUTIES AND IMPOSTS, LAID BY ANY STATE ON IMPORTS OR EXPORTS, SHALL BE FOR THE USE OF THE TREASURY OF THE UNITED STATES; AND ALL SUCH LAWS SHALL BE SUBJECT TO THE REVISION AND CONTROL OF THE CONGRESS.

Inspection laws determine whether or not any commodity intended for market is of such condition or quality as to be suitable for use or consumption. For example, the courts have held that a fee for storage and inspection of every hogshead of tobacco intended for export was an inspection law legitimately levied by a state. Congress, of course, has power to supervise such laws. All other taxes by individual states upon imports and exports require congressional approval and the money so collected goes into the national treasury.

Clause 3. <u>Entering into Compacts and Agreements</u>

> NO STATE SHALL, WITHOUT THE CONSENT OF CONGRESS, LAY ANY DUTY OF TONNAGE, KEEP TROOPS, OR SHIPS OF WAR IN TIME OF PEACE, ENTER INTO ANY AGREEMENT OR COMPACT WITH ANOTHER STATE, OR WITH A FOREIGN POWER, OR ENGAGE IN WAR, UNLESS ACTUALLY INVADED, OR IN SUCH IMMINENT DANGER AS WILL NOT ADMIT OF DELAY.

A tonnage duty is a charge for the privilege of entering, trading in, or lying in a port. A state tax for pilot or towage service is perfectly valid.

This clause prohibits a permanent or large-scale military establishment. State militia or national guards are permitted. A state cannot declare war. An invasion of a state is also an invasion of the United States; therefore the national government would be automatically involved.

Agreements and compacts, as used in this clause, do not mean the same things as treaties that states are absolutely forbidden to enter into with foreign nations. With congressional approval, states may enter into a variety of agreements among themselves. For years these were mainly concerned with boundary settlements. In recent years the states have used the interstate compact as a means of solving and administering common problems. There are in existence compacts that relate to tobacco production, flood control, conservation, fishing, natural gas, pollution on rivers, and harbor facilities. Congress may give its approval before the agreement is made or afterward. Its approval may be expressed openly or may be assumed from its inaction. Reciprocity agreements among the states do not have to get congressional approval. That is, Pennsylvania may permit doctors or lawyers licensed in another state to practice in Pennsylvania, in return for the same privilege accorded doctors and lawyers licensed by Pennsylvania.

Article II

The Executive

Section 1   Powers of the President

Clause 1. The Executive Power

> THE EXECUTIVE POWER SHALL BE VESTED IN A PRESIDENT OF THE UNITED STATES OF AMERICA. HE SHALL HOLD THIS OFFICE DURING THE TERM OF FOUR YEARS, AND, TOGETHER WITH THE VICE PRESIDENT, CHOSEN FOR THE SAME TERM, BE ELECTED, AS FOLLOWS:

Notice the difference in language between this clause and the first clause of the legislative Article. Compare "the executive power shall be vested in a President" with "all legislative power *herein granted* shall be vested in a Congress." The executive power is not modified or confined to only those specific powers that follow. This means that the President possesses vast and general powers that have never been defined in the Constitution. It means that he can draw upon a vast reservoir of authority to sustain actions that defy exact enumeration in the Constitution. These vast "executive powers" provide, in part, the basis for proclamations, for Jefferson's embargoes, for Lincoln's blockade, and for Franklin Roosevelt's executive agreements. President Nixon's claim of executive privilege in refusing to turn over the so-called Watergate tapes to either the special prosecutor or the Senate investigating committee was based, in part, on this clause. However, in the unique case of *United States of America v. Richard M. Nixon, President et al* (1974), the Court ruled that President Nixon's claim of executive privilege to assure the confidentiality of information cannot be used to withhold material vital to criminal proceedings. The Court did give some credence to the concept of a qualified executive privilege, especially in the area of policy alternatives.

In another facet of what the Supreme Court called "the president's unique office, rooted in the constitutional tradition," a bare majority of the justices ruled on June 24, 1982, that a current or former president (in this case, Richard M. Nixon) "is entitled to absolute immunity from damages liability predicated on his official acts." However, in a related 8–1 decision, the Court also ruled that a president's closest advisers are entitled to only a "qualified immunity." The President, therefore, does not have unlimited power since both these 1982 cases emphasized that there was an "outer perimeter" beyond which the immunity does not extend. Thus the President must also be guided by the constitutional system, as are the legislature and the courts.

Clause 2. Presidential Elections

> EACH STATE SHALL APPOINT, IN SUCH MANNER AS THE LEGISLATURE THEREOF MAY DIRECT, A NUMBER OF ELECTORS, EQUAL TO THE WHOLE NUMBER OF SENATORS AND REPRESENTATIVES TO WHICH THE STATE MAY BE ENTITLED IN THE CONGRESS: BUT NO SENATOR OR REPRESENTATIVE, OR PERSON HOLDING AN OFFICE OF TRUST OR PROFIT UNDER THE UNITED STATES, SHALL BE APPOINTED AN ELECTOR.

Using this constitutional power, state legislatures have enacted a number of methods for selecting electors. At some time or other in our history they have been selected by state legislatures, elected by voters in congressional districts, or elected by all the voters in the state.

Today presidential electors in every state except Maine are elected by the voters of the entire state under what is called a *general-ticket* system. If a presidential candidate wins the popular vote of a state, even by only one vote, all the electors pledged to him and his party are elected. Under such a system, it is an all-or-nothing proposition. For example, President John F. Kennedy carried Illinois by fewer than 9,000 votes in 1960, yet he received that state's twenty-seven electoral votes. In Maine, voters in each of the state's two congressional districts elect one elector, and the state-wide vote total determines which candidate wins the two at-large elector posts.

Clause 2. [*continued*] Meeting of Electors

THE ELECTORS SHALL MEET IN THEIR RESPECTIVE STATES, AND VOTE BY BALLOT FOR TWO PERSONS, OF WHOM ONE AT LEAST SHALL NOT BE AN INHABITANT OF THE SAME STATE WITH THEMSELVES. AND THEY SHALL MAKE A LIST OF ALL THE PERSONS VOTED FOR, AND THE NUMBER OF VOTES FOR EACH; WHICH LIST THEY SHALL SIGN AND CERTIFY, AND TRANSMIT SEALED TO THE PRESIDENT OF THE SENATE. THE PRESIDENT OF THE SENATE SHALL, IN THE PRESENCE OF THE SENATE AND HOUSE OF REPRESENTATIVES, OPEN ALL THE CERTIFICATES, AND THE VOTES SHALL THEN BE COUNTED. THE PERSON HAVING THE GREATEST NUMBER OF VOTES SHALL THEN BE PRESIDENT, IF SUCH NUMBER BE A MAJORITY OF THE WHOLE NUMBER OF ELECTORS APPOINTED; AND IF THERE BE MORE THAN ONE WHO HAVE SUCH MAJORITY AND HAVE AN EQUAL NUMBER OF VOTES, THEN THE HOUSE OF REPRESENTATIVES SHALL IMMEDIATELY CHOOSE BY BALLOT ONE OF THEM FOR PRESIDENT; AND IF NO PERSON HAVE A MAJORITY, THEN FROM THE FIVE HIGHEST ON THE LIST THE SAID HOUSE SHALL IN LIKE MANNER CHOOSE THE PRESIDENT. BUT IN CHOOSING THE PRESIDENT, THE VOTES SHALL BE TAKEN BY STATES, THE REPRESENTATION FROM EACH STATE HAVING ONE VOTE; A QUORUM FOR THIS PURPOSE SHALL CONSIST OF A MEMBER OR MEMBERS FROM TWO THIRDS OF THE STATES, AND A MAJORITY OF ALL THE STATES SHALL BE NECESSARY TO A CHOICE. IN EVERY CASE, AFTER THE CHOICE OF THE PRESIDENT, THE PERSON HAVING THE GREATEST NUMBER OF VOTES OF THE ELECTORS SHALL BE THE VICE PRESIDENT. BUT IF THERE SHOULD REMAIN TWO OR MORE WHO HAVE EQUAL VOTES, THE SENATE SHALL CHOOSE FROM THEM BY BALLOT THE VICE PRESIDENT.

This entire clause has been replaced by the Twelfth Amendment. A number of the framers of the Constitution believed that the House of Representatives would make the final selection of the President in nine elections out of ten. They reasoned that the state legislatures would, by various methods, select their most outstanding men as electors. These electors would cast their individual votes for presidential candidates. In an era where state loyalty and pride ran to extremes, it was felt that the electoral votes would be split among a great many candidates. It was thought that each elector would cast at least one vote for someone from his own state. Thus no one candidate would receive a majority of the electoral votes and the House of Representatives would select a President from the top five candidates. The candidate with the next highest number of votes would become Vice-President.

This system worked satisfactorily for the first three elections. By 1800, however, political parties were well organized. The parties put up electors who were pledged to support their party's candidates. The function of the electoral college became largely that of a rubber stamp—ratifying the results of the popular election. In 1800 the system further broke down when Jefferson and Aaron Burr, although from the same party, received the same number of electoral votes. The Twelfth Amendment was proposed so that the electors would distinguish their votes for President from that of Vice-President.

Clause 3. Casting Electoral Votes

THE CONGRESS MAY DETERMINE THE TIME OF CHOOSING THE ELECTORS, AND THE DAY ON WHICH THEY SHALL GIVE THEIR VOTES; WHICH DAY SHALL BE THE SAME THROUGHOUT THE UNITED STATES.

Presidential electors are chosen on the first Tuesday after the first Monday in November. Actually we elect our President and Vice-President on this day because electors are pledged to vote for their party's candidates.

On the first Monday after the second Wednesday in December the presidential electors meet, usually at their respective state capitols, and cast their electoral votes. Six lists of the electoral votes are prepared and distributed as follows: one to the president of the Senate, two to the Administrator of General Services, two to the Secretary of State of their respective states, and one to the federal district court in whose jurisdiction the meeting took place. Congress was making sure that no state's electoral vote would get lost or misplaced.

On January 6 the president of the Senate opens the certificates before a joint session of Congress. Aided by one member of the Senate and one from the House of Representatives, he tabulates the electoral votes and announces the result. The people, however, have known the outcome since the morning after the election.

Clause 4. Qualifications for President

> NO PERSON EXCEPT A NATURAL BORN CITIZEN, OR A CITIZEN OF THE UNITED STATES, AT THE TIME OF THE ADOPTION OF THIS CONSTITUTION, SHALL BE ELIGIBLE TO THE OFFICE OF PRESIDENT; NEITHER SHALL ANY PERSON BE ELIGIBLE TO THAT OFFICE WHO SHALL NOT HAVE ATTAINED THE AGE OF THIRTY FIVE YEARS, AND BEEN FOURTEEN YEARS A RESIDENT WITHIN THE UNITED STATES.

This clause is mainly of historical interest. All Presidents after William Henry Harrison have been born in the United States. There is a question whether a child born to American parents in a foreign country is a "natural-born" citizen within the meaning of this clause. Such a child would, of course, be an American citizen, but could he ever become President? The answer to this question will have to await an actual case wherein the Supreme Court must interpret the meaning of "natural-born" citizen.

President Herbert Hoover's election in 1928 removed the constitutional doubt concerning the fourteen year residence requirement. He had been out of the country a good deal of the time but no doubt was raised about his election on residential grounds. Thus the fourteen years means a total of fourteen years and not fourteen consecutive years.

Clause 5. <u>Death, Removal, or Inability of President to Serve</u>

IN CASE OF THE REMOVAL OF THE PRESIDENT FROM OFFICE, OR OF HIS DEATH, RESIGNATION, OR INABILITY TO DISCHARGE THE POWERS AND DUTIES OF THE SAID OFFICE, THE SAME SHALL DEVOLVE ON THE VICE PRESIDENT, AND THE CONGRESS MAY BY LAW PROVIDE FOR THE CASE OF REMOVAL, DEATH, RESIGNATION, OR INABILITY, BOTH OF THE PRESIDENT, AND VICE PRESIDENT, DECLARING WHAT OFFICER SHALL THEN ACT AS PRESIDENT, AND SUCH OFFICER SHALL ACT ACCORDINGLY, UNTIL THE DISABILITY BE REMOVED, OR A PRESIDENT SHALL BE ELECTED.

In 1841, William H. Harrison was the first President to die while in office. Doubt existed as to whether the Vice-President would "act" as President or whether he succeeded to the title as well. John Tyler, the Vice-President, settled the question then and for all time by assuming the title of President as well as the "powers and duties" of that office. Since Tyler's time seven other Vice-Presidents have succeeded to the presidency upon the death of the incumbent. Vice-President Gerald R. Ford succeeded to the presidency on August 9, 1974, upon the resignation of President Nixon—the only such occasion in our history.

Upon the inability of the President to discharge the powers and duties of his office, the Vice-President "acts" as President. A serious gap existed in our law until 1967, when the Twenty-Fifth Amendment set up a procedure for determining a president's disability. Certainly the Vice-President cannot take it upon himself to decide whether the President is so ill as to be unable to carry on the duties of his office. It is a real problem because we have had such instances in our history. President James Garfield lived seventy-nine days after an assassin shot him down in 1881. Woodrow Wilson suffered a paralyzing breakdown for several months during his second term. President Eisenhower's illnesses resulted in a private understanding between him and Vice-President Nixon on the procedure for the latter's assumption of presidential duties in case of the President's disability. The constitutionality of this private agreement was questioned by some authorities. A similar agreement existed between President Kennedy and Vice-President Johnson.

In the event of death, resignation, removal, or disability of the President *and* the Vice-President, Congress has prescribed by law a line of succession to the presidency. First is the Speaker of the House of Representatives, then the President pro tempore of the Senate, next the Secretary of State, followed by other cabinet officers in the order that their departments were established. A person succeeding under this law must, of course, possess all the constitutional qualifications of a President. Also, the successor must resign his congressional seat or cabinet position, whichever the case may be, before assuming the office of President.

Clause 6. Compensation

> THE PRESIDENT SHALL, AT STATED TIMES, RECEIVE FOR HIS SERVICES, A COMPENSATION, WHICH SHALL NEITHER BE INCREASED NOR DIMINISHED DURING THE PERIOD FOR WHICH HE SHALL HAVE BEEN ELECTED, AND HE SHALL NOT RECEIVE WITHIN THAT PERIOD ANY OTHER EMOLUMENT FROM THE UNITED STATES, OR ANY OF THEM.

This clause prevents Congress from influencing the President by means of salary cuts or promises of pay increases. This clause is similar to one found in Article III which protects the independence of federal judges. Furthermore, the President is free of any dependency upon the states, particularly his own state.

The President's salary is now fixed by Congress at $200,000 per year. In addition he receives an allowance of $100,000 each year for traveling expenses plus $50,000 per year for general expenses. The President's salary and general expense account are taxable. In addition, there are other privileges that go with the office such as: free use of the White House, private plane, summer or vacation quarters, professional and secretarial assistance, and a number of other items. A former president receives a pension equal to the salary of the head of a cabinet department ($148,400 in 1993).

Clause 7. Oath of Office

> BEFORE HE ENTER ON THE EXECUTION OF HIS OFFICE, HE SHALL TAKE THIS FOLLOWING OATH OR AFFIRMATION:—"I DO SOLEMNLY SWEAR (OR AFFIRM) THAT I WILL FAITHFULLY EXECUTE THE OFFICE OF PRESIDENT OF THE UNITED STATES, AND WILL TO THE BEST OF MY ABILITY, PRESERVE, PROTECT AND DEFEND THE CONSTITUTION OF THE UNITED STATES."

Any judicial officer may administer the oath of office, though the Chief Justice of the Supreme Court usually performs this duty during an elaborate ceremony on Inauguration Day, now January 20. There is the sentimental incident in American history of Calvin Coolidge being sworn into office by his father, a Justice of the Peace in Vermont, after the death of Warren Harding in 1923.

Section 2   Powers of the President

Clause 1. Commander in Chief

> THE PRESIDENT SHALL BE COMMANDER IN CHIEF OF THE ARMY AND NAVY OF THE UNITED STATES AND OF THE MILITIA OF THE SEVERAL STATES, WHEN CALLED INTO THE ACTUAL SERVICE OF THE UNITED STATES.

In keeping with the American tradition of the supremacy of the civilian over the military, the President is made the commander in chief of our armed forces. It is unlikely that he would ever take active field command, but the Constitution would not prevent him from so doing. He does, of course, appoint military officers, subject to the Senate's approval.

Although commander in chief, the President does not possess unlimited control over the armed forces. Congress has a good deal to say through its control over finances and its power to "declare war." The President may send U.S. forces anywhere in the world and perhaps bring about a situation where Congress has no choice but to "declare war." The Mexican War in 1848 was brought about, in part, through President Polk's order to send troops into disputed areas.

This clause has been used by several presidents as a means of exercising power in areas that were not strictly military. During the Civil War, President Lincoln based his action of increasing the number of members in the regular army on this clause. Also, the basis of the Emancipation Proclamation was this clause. President Franklin D. Roosevelt used it several times in dealing with emergency situations, particularly during World War II. However, the clause does not justify any and all actions taken by a president during a crisis. When President Truman ordered the seizure of the steel industry during the Korean War in 1952, the Supreme Court declared his action unconstitutional. The shadowy area of the President's war powers is illustrated by both congressional and popular reaction to the commitment of military forces in the Vietnam War by a succession of presidents; President Gerald Ford's handling of the Mayaguez incident in 1975; and President Carter's actions relative to the Iranian hostage crisis of 1979–1980. Another dimension of the president's "war powers" was cast by the all-out debate in Congress over U.S. commitments to the Desert Storm (Iraq) engagement in 1991 under President George Bush and the apparent muddled nature of the response to the Bosnia crisis in 1993 during President Clinton's watch.

Clause 1. [*continued*] Administrative Powers

HE MAY REQUIRE THE OPINION, IN WRITING, OF THE PRINCIPAL OFFICER IN EACH OF THE EXECUTIVE DEPARTMENTS, UPON ANY SUBJECT RELATING TO THE DUTIES OF THEIR RESPECTIVE OFFICES.

This clause is the basis of the *Cabinet* as we know it today. Notice that the term cabinet is nowhere mentioned in the Constitution, here or elsewhere.

The concept of the President conferring and consulting with a small group of advisers stems from this power to require written reports. Early in Washington's administration this custom developed and today it is a well-established feature of our government.

The President, of course, appoints the heads of the departments and may remove them at any time. He alone calls Cabinet meetings, usually one a week, though sometimes more frequently during times of emergency. The President may invite anyone to these meetings, but they are usually confined to the fourteen executive department heads and the Vice-President. The President may make as much or as little use of the Cabinet as he desires. There may sometimes be actual votes in the Cabinet on an issue, but the President is bound neither by a vote nor by any individual member's advice.

Clause 1. [*continued*] Clemency Powers

AND HE SHALL HAVE POWER TO GRANT REPRIEVES AND PARDONS FOR OFFENCES AGAINST THE UNITED STATES, EXCEPT IN CASES OF IMPEACHMENT.

A *pardon* exempts a person from the punishment a law prescribes for a crime. It usually restores to a person his legal and political rights. A *reprieve* merely postpones the execution of a punishment. Included within the President's pardoning power are two other clemency powers: *amnesty,* which is a pardon to a group, and *commutation,* which substitutes a lesser penalty for a greater one (commute a death sentence to life imprisonment).

Notice that the President may pardon only for offenses committed against the United States. A person sentenced to death by a state court for murder could not be pardoned by the President. Also, the President's power to pardon does not apply to persons convicted of impeachment. The President may, however, extend a pardon at any time *after* the commission of a crime, or even alleged crime, as in the case of President Ford's pardon of Richard M. Nixon. The same holds true for President Bush's pardon of former Secretary of Defense Caspar W. Weinberger in December, 1992, before Weinberger's trial had even begun.

Clause 2. Treaty-Making Power

HE SHALL HAVE POWER, BY AND WITH THE ADVICE AND
CONSENT OF THE SENATE, TO MAKE TREATIES, PROVIDED TWO
THIRDS OF THE SENATORS PRESENT CONCUR;

The President negotiates treaties. Actually the Secretary of State, acting under the President's general instructions, confers, discusses, and reaches agreements with foreign leaders. The President must submit the treaty to the Senate for its approval. The Senate may approve of the treaty unconditionally (i.e., without changes), it may make amendments, or it may make reservations to the agreement. The Senate may also reject a treaty, in which case it does not become law. A two-thirds vote is necessary to approve a treaty. This means two-thirds of the Senators present, provided a quorum exists.

If the Senate approves unconditionally, it forwards the treaty to the President for his signature. This is called *ratification.* A treaty so approved and signed becomes a part of the law of the United States and is enforced by our courts.

If the Senate approves with ammendments, then the President must submit it to the other nation involved for its approval of the Senate's amendments. If the other nation accepts, then the President may sign the treaty and it likewise becomes law in the United States.

If the Senate approves with reservations, these then limit only the obligations of the United States under the treaty and do not affect the other party or parties. Of course, the President may refuse to submit a treaty to the other parties if the Senate adds amendments or reservations. In this case, the treaty does not become law.

The two-thirds vote requirement has sometimes meant the downfall of treaties. Certain sectional or political groupings in the Senate may control over one-third of the votes and secure a defeat. In order to evade a possible hostile minority, two devices have developed over the years. One is the *joint resolution* which merely requires a majority vote in each house. Both Texas and Hawaii were annexed in this fashion because the necessary two-thirds vote was lacking for a treaty. The second method is the *executive agreement.* This is an arrangement whereby the President may enter into an agreement with foreign governments without having to submit the results to the Senate. The President's authority to enter into such agreements comes from two sources: (1) from powers given to him by Congress. For example, Congress passed the Reciprocal Trade Agreements Act which set down the general tariff policy. Congress then permits the president to make specific agreements with foreign countries regarding this policy. (2) from his powers as chief executive plus his position as the sole spokesman for the United States in international affairs. This second source of authority is more definite. Acting in these capacities, in addition to that of commander in chief, President Franklin D. Roosevelt made an agreement with the British in 1940. In exchange for fifty overage destroyers the United States received ninety-nine year leases for military bases on British-owned land in the Western Hemisphere. However, after worsening relations between the President and Congress over foreign affairs, especially Vietnam, Congress passed a law that directed the Secretary of State to send Congress or its Foreign Affairs Committees the text of any agreement, other than a treaty, with another country.

Clause 2. [*continued*] Appointing Power

AND HE SHALL NOMINATE, AND BY AND WITH THE ADVICE AND CONSENT OF THE SENATE, SHALL APPOINT AMBASSADORS, OTHER PUBLIC MINISTERS AND CONSULS, JUDGES OF THE SUPREME COURT, AND ALL OTHER OFFICERS OF THE UNITED STATES, WHOSE APPOINTMENTS ARE NOT HEREIN OTHERWISE PROVIDED FOR, AND WHICH SHALL BE ESTABLISHED BY LAW: BUT THE CONGRESS MAY BY LAW VEST THE APPOINTMENT OF SUCH INFERIOR OFFICERS, AS THEY THINK PROPER, IN THE PRESIDENT ALONE, IN THE COURTS OF LAW, OR IN THE HEADS OF DEPARTMENTS.

Except for the President and Vice-President, all the other officers in our federal executive and administrative branch are appointed. These officers fall into three groups:

(1) *Superior officer(s)* are appointed by the President and subject

to the Senate's approval. These would include diplomats and military officers, members of boards, agencies, and commissions, heads of departments, and their chief assistants.

(2) *Inferior officers,* appointed either by the President, courts of law, or heads of departments, usually require no senatorial approval. They would include such officers as bureau chiefs, clerks of courts, and various types of specialists.

(3) *Employees* are appointed by subordinate officials and do not require senatorial approval. The majority of persons in this category are usually covered by civil service regulations.

In approving appointments the Senate exercises a restraining influence over the President. A custom has developed whereby a Senator of the President's political party may object to a federal appointment to be made in his state. The rest of the Senate will go along with this objection by refusing to approve the appointment. This is called *senatorial courtesy.* In 1951 and again in 1952 President Truman (D) nominated three men as judges to the federal district court in Chicago. Senator Paul Douglas (D-IL), objected to two of the appointees. Therefore the Senate refused to confirm the appointments. Neither President Truman nor Senator Douglas would back down, and so the vacancies remained until the Republican administration took over in 1953. Senator Douglas, of course, could no longer exercise the privilege, but Senator Everett Dirkson (R-IL) passed upon appointments to be made in Illinois.

After the Senate has notified the President of its approval it may not reconsider nor rescind the appointment.

Clause 3. Power to Fill Vacancies

THE PRESIDENT SHALL HAVE POWER TO FILL UP ALL VACANCIES THAT MAY HAPPEN DURING THE RECESS OF THE SENATE, BY GRANTING COMMISSIONS WHICH SHALL EXPIRE AT THE END OF THEIR NEXT SESSION.

Through constitutional interpretation this clause allows the President to fill any vacancy by a temporary appointment while the

Senate is not in session. This type of an appointment is called a *recess appointment.* If the Senate does not approve of the appointment before it adjourns in the next session, then the person appointed loses his position. The President also has the power to make temporary or *ad interim* appointments of officials who perform the duties of other absent officials.

Section 3   Legislative Powers of the President

Clause 1. <u>Messages to Congress</u>

> HE SHALL FROM TIME TO TIME GIVE TO THE CONGRESS INFORMATION OF THE STATE OF THE UNION, AND RECOMMEND TO THEIR CONSIDERATION SUCH MEASURES AS HE SHALL JUDGE NECESSARY AND EXPEDIENT.

This clause introduces the President's so-called legislative power. Shortly after Congress convenes each year the President sends a message known as the State of the Union message. This address usually recounts the accomplishments of his administration and sets forth in broad outlines the policies and programs he intends to follow in the year ahead. Recent practice has revived the precedent of Washington and John Adams by delivering this message in person before a joint meeting of the two houses. A few days after the State of the Union message, the President transmits a budget message and an economic report to Congress.

Throughout an entire session a President constantly forwards messages or makes appeals to Congress for the passage of particular legislation. In this way the President lays before Congress, and the people of the United States, his specific plans and proposals for carrying out the policies announced in his State of the Union message.

Clause 1. [*continued*] <u>Call Special Sessions of Congress</u>

> HE MAY, ON EXTRAORDINARY OCCASIONS, CONVENE BOTH HOUSES, OR EITHER OF THEM,

This clause gives the President the power to call special sessions of Congress. He alone determines the need for such a meeting. But once called for, Congress possesses its full powers. It may stay in session as long as it desires and transact any and all of its legislative business.

The likelihood of calling the House into a special session alone is very remote. The Senate, however, has been called a number of times for the purpose of approving treaties or confirming appointments. Usually both houses are called. The Twentieth Amendment, by eliminating the short "lame duck" session, has lessened the need for special sessions.

Clause 1. [*continued*] Adjourn Congress

> AND IN CASE OF DISAGREEMENT BETWEEN THEM, WITH RESPECT TO THE TIME OF ADJOURNMENT, HE MAY ADJOURN THEM TO SUCH TIME AS HE SHALL THINK PROPER.

This has never happened in the history of the U.S. government. There are several instances wherein state governors have exercised a similar power over their state legislatures.

Clause 1. [*continued*] Receive Foreign Representatives

> HE SHALL RECEIVE AMBASSADORS AND OTHER PUBLIC MINISTERS;

The President is the sole official spokesman for the United States in its dealings with foreign countries. Also, he is the only authority through which foreign nations channel their dealings with the United States. In practice, of course, the Secretary of State is the nominal agency for handling foreign affairs. This power to "receive" diplomatic officials also includes the right to refuse to receive or to request the recall of a foreign representative. In addition, the "receiving" power together with other constitutional powers, gives the President authority to recognize new foreign governments. For example, when Juan Peron was ousted as president of Argentina in 1955, the new regime was recognized by the U.S. government almost immediately.

Clause 1. [*continued*] Execute the Laws

> HE SHALL TAKE CARE THAT THE LAWS BE FAITHFULLY EXECUTED, AND SHALL COMMISSION ALL THE OFFICERS OF THE UNITED STATES.

The President does not execute all the laws himself. This clause empowers him to make sure his subordinates faithfully enforce the laws. In order to make this supervisory task of the President effective, he possesses the power to remove subordinate officials. For just "cause" or reason he may institute removal proceedings against any executive or administrative official, even those under civil service. On his own authority he may remove certain executive officials for purely political reasons. For example, in 1946 President Truman removed Harry Wallace as Secretary of Commerce because of political differences. Other officials, particularly those engaged in "quasi-legislative" and "quasi-judicial" functions, such as the Interstate Commerce Commission or the Federal Trade Commission, cannot be removed for political reasons.

In faithfully executing the laws, the President may call upon the other branches of the government for assistance and even use the military forces. In 1794 Washington sent the militia into western Pennsylvania in order to quell a domestic uprising which prevented the enforcement of a tax law. Since then there have been numerous instances where the President has had to call upon the military to execute the laws of the United States, the most recent being the use of federal troops in Little Rock, Arkansas, in 1957 and in Oxford, Mississippi, in 1962, to enforce federal court decisions on integration of schools.

Various presidents have "impounded" funds that have been appropriated by Congress for particular purposes. Because legislators believed the President was abusing this practice, Congress passed the Congressional Budget and Impoundment Control Act of 1974. Under this law, presidential impoundment of funds, either temporarily or permanently, is prohibited unless Congress specifically gives permission. Typically, when a situation appears to be unbalanced, lower federal courts are beginning to restrict the so-called congressional veto.

Section 4   Impeachment of Civil Officers

THE PRESIDENT, VICE PRESIDENT, AND ALL CIVIL OFFICERS OF THE UNITED STATES, SHALL BE REMOVED FROM OFFICE ON IMPEACHMENT FOR, AND CONVICTION OF, TREASON, BRIBERY, OR OTHER HIGH CRIMES AND MISDEMEANORS.

A private citizen cannot be impeached. Military personnel come under their court-martial procedure rather than impeachment. Early in our history it was established that members of Congress do not come within the impeachment clause. They are subject to removal by a two-thirds vote of expulsion from their respective houses. Therefore the impeachment process applies only to executive and judicial officers.

The House of Representatives impeaches (i.e., accuses), and the Senate tries the case. A resignation by an official does not bar later impeachment proceedings for offenses committed while he was in office. This is rarely done however. Upon President Nixon's resignation in 1974, the House of Representatives voted to accept its Judiciary Committee's Impeachment Report and dropped all further impeachment proceedings. The penalty attached to conviction does not prevent further trial in the regular courts if the offense was of a criminal nature.

Treason and bribery are well understood terms. But "high crimes and misdemeanors" present a problem. Fortunately for the United States, these terms came to mean any indictable offense. Thus the impeachment procedure has not been used as a partisan device to remove objectionable or unpopular officials.

Article III

The Judicial Branch

Section 1   Federal Courts and Judges

THE JUDICIAL POWER OF THE UNITED STATES, SHALL BE VESTED IN ONE SUPREME COURT, AND IN SUCH INFERIOR COURTS AS THE CONGRESS MAY FROM TIME TO TIME ORDAIN AND ESTABLISH. THE JUDGES, BOTH OF THE SUPREME AND INFERIOR COURTS, SHALL HOLD THEIR OFFICES DURING GOOD BEHAVIOR, AND SHALL, AT STATED TIMES, RECEIVE FOR THEIR SERVICES, A COMPENSATION, WHICH SHALL NOT BE DIMINISHED DURING THEIR CONTINUANCE IN OFFICE.

This section provides the basis for our elaborate federal judicial system. Note how vague and general the framers were in creating the judicial department. Only one court is specifically mentioned—the Supreme Court. Not a word is said about the size, composition, procedure, or internal organization of the federal courts. These matters, like the establishment of inferior courts, are left to the determination of Congress.

Before attempting to describe the courts and their duties, an understanding of a few legal terms is necessary. This article begins with the words "judicial power." This means the power of a court to hear and pronounce a judgment and carry that judgment into effect. Another familiar legal term is "jurisdiction." This is the authority of a court to exercise judicial power in a specific case. There are two kinds of jurisdiction, original and appellate. *Original jurisdiction* means the power of a court to hear and decide cases in the first instance. That is to say, the case begins in this court. *Appellate jurisdiction* is the power to hear and decide cases started in a lower court but which have been appealed to the higher court. Congress determines the jurisdiction of the several courts.

There are two kinds of federal courts. *Constitutional courts* are those established by this article of the Constitution and include the

Supreme Court, the Courts of Appeals, the District Courts, the Court of Customs and Patent Appeals, the Court of Claims, and the Customs Court. *Legislative courts* are those which have been established by Congress under powers given to it by other sections of the Constitution (Article I, Section 8). Congress's power over the armed services gives it the implied power to establish a Court of Military Appeals. Other legislative courts are: the District Court of Puerto Rico and territorial courts. The courts of the District of Columbia are both constitutional and legislative, just to confuse things still further. Congress has considerably more control over legislative courts in the way of jurisdiction, fixing salaries, and tenure than it possesses over constitutional courts.

The *Supreme Court* is the highest court in the land. Its decision is final on any case coming within its jurisdiction. At the present time there are nine justices on the Supreme Court, although its size has ranged from as few as five to as many as ten. All justices, or as many as are able, hear each case. No jury is used by this court. The justices listen to oral arguments, read the written briefs, hold conferences, and finally vote on each case. The majority of those participating determines the disposition of the case.

The *Courts of Appeals,* of which there are thirteen located throughout the country, stand immediately below the Supreme Court. Their main function is to act as a sort of buffer or screen for the Supreme Court. If the Supreme Court had to hear all the cases arising under federal judicial power, it would be years behind its schedule. This is where the Courts of Appeals step in and relieve the higher court of some of the burden of cases. The Courts of Appeals hear appeals from District Courts, some legislative courts, and certain administrative agencies. They are strictly appellate courts; one would never start a case in the Courts of Appeals. A few classes of cases may be taken up to the Supreme Court on appeal from the Courts of Appeals, but the bulk of the cases terminate at this level. Each Court of Appeal has at least three judges, though more may be added because of the volume of business. At least two judges are required to hear a case. Like the Supreme Court, this Court does not employ a jury.

The bottom rung of the judicial ladder is occupied by the 94 *District Courts.* Nearly all the cases involving federal law begin at this level because it is the court of original jurisdiction. In fact, it has no appellate jurisdiction. There is at least one District Court in each state (and most territories), and each court has at least one judge. But again, more courts and judges may be added because of the amount of litigation. The jury is used in the District Courts.

All federal judges are appointed by the President and confirmed by the Senate. Surprisingly there are no qualifications listed for federal judges, as there are for other federal officials. Judges are appointed to indefinite terms on "good behavior." Since impeachment has proved almost impossible, Congress, in 1980, set up a system within the federal judiciary to deal with disabled or incompetent judges, short of removal. Judges' salaries in 1993 ranged from $164,100 for Supreme Court justices ($171,500 for the Chief Justice), $141,700 for Appellate judges, and $133,600 for District Court judges. This salary cannot be decreased during a judge's term of office, although it may be increased. The reason for this stipulation is to protect the independence of the judicial branch from Congress's power of the purse. It is customary, as you have noticed, to speak of a Supreme Court member as "justice," while referring to other federal judicial officials as "judge."

Section 2   Jurisdiction of the Federal Courts

Clause 1. Types of Cases and Controversies

> THE JUDICIAL POWER SHALL EXTEND TO ALL CASES, IN LAW AND EQUITY, ARISING UNDER THIS CONSTITUTION, THE LAWS OF THE UNITED STATES, AND TREATIES MADE, OR WHICH SHALL BE MADE, UNDER THEIR AUTHORITY;

This section deals with the types of cases and controversies with which the federal courts will be involved. First of all, these courts will not handle a hypothetical case. Neither will they give an advisory opinion, as some state courts have the authority to do. The suit must be real and involve adverse parties. Second, the courts hear suits "in law and equity" which are systems of law originating in England centuries ago. The "law" refers to common law under which a person brings suit for damages for an injury already done to him or his property. Under "equity," on the other hand, a person seeks to prevent an injury from being done by means of injunctions or other court orders.

Cases arising under the Constitution, national laws, and treaties are those which require the Court to interpret the Constitution in order to render a decision. Thus, if a person claims a constitutional right has been infringed upon by either a national or state law, he may petition the courts to interpret the law in accordance with what the Constitution says. If there is no conflict between the law and the Constitution, the law is valid and may be enforced. If, however, there is a conflict, the Constitution, being superior to all other law, is applied and the law becomes null and void, i.e., unconstitutional. This, in brief, is the great doctrine of *judicial review* which was discussed in Chapter Two.

Clause 1. [*continued*] Diplomatic Cases

TO ALL CASES AFFECTING AMBASSADORS, OTHER PUBLIC MINISTERS AND CONSULS;

This clause has reference to suits involving foreign ambassadors, ministers, and consuls. Certain types of actions affecting these persons, such as divorce, may be brought in the state courts.

Clause 1. [*continued*] Admiralty and Maritime Cases

ALL CASES OF ADMIRALTY AND MARITIME JURISDICTION;

Technically *admiralty* refers to police regulations of a local nature—harbor, fishing, etc., regulations—and *maritime* deals with cases arising upon the oceans. In the United States the "admiralty and maritime" jurisdictions have been interpreted so as to give the national government considerable control over all navigable waters, which includes large lakes and rivers, as well as ocean water. This jurisdiction of the courts also covers contracts and other transactions connected with shipping.

Clause 1. [*continued*] Cases Involving the United States and States

> TO CONTROVERSIES TO WHICH THE UNITED STATES SHALL BE A PARTY, TO CONTROVERSIES BETWEEN TWO OR MORE STATES.

It is a well-established principle of law that the "sovereign cannot be sued in his own courts." Thus the U.S. government cannot be sued unless Congress gives permission—which it has by providing a general scheme for suing the government. The United States, however, may sue any individual, or even a state, without their approval. Disputes between states are heard in the Supreme Court.

Clause 1. [*continued*] Cases Involving States

> BETWEEN A STATE AND CITIZENS OF ANOTHER STATE, BETWEEN CITIZENS OF DIFFERENT STATES.

The underlined portion has been modified by the Eleventh Amendment. The clause is the basis of a great deal of litigation and is often called the "diversity of citizenship" clause. The framers put this into the Constitution in order to prevent a state court from favoring its own citizens over citizens of other states. Cases involving $50,000 or less must begin in the state courts.

Clause 1. [*continued*] Cases Involving Land Grants

> BETWEEN CITIZENS OF THE SAME STATE CLAIMING LANDS UNDER GRANTS OF DIFFERENT STATES.

This clause has little significance today. At the time of the drafting of the Constitution certain western lands were claimed by persons who had received or bought them from different states.

Clause 1. [*continued*] <u>Cases Between Citizens of Different States</u>

> BETWEEN A STATE, OR THE CITIZENS THEREOF, AND FOREIGN
> STATES, CITIZENS OR SUBJECTS.

This clause was also modified by the Eleventh Amendment. A citizen of a foreign nation, or a foreign government itself, may not sue a state in the federal courts without that state's consent.

Clause 2. <u>Original and Appellate Jurisdiction of Supreme Court</u>

> IN ALL CASES AFFECTING AMBASSADORS, OTHER PUBLIC
> MINISTERS AND CONSULS, AND THOSE IN WHICH A STATE SHALL
> BE A PARTY, THE SUPREME COURT SHALL HAVE ORIGINAL
> JURISDICTION. IN ALL THE OTHER CASES BEFORE MENTIONED, THE
> SUPREME COURT SHALL HAVE APPELLATE JURISDICTION, BOTH AS
> TO LAW AND FACT, WITH SUCH EXCEPTIONS, AND UNDER SUCH
> REGULATIONS AS THE CONGRESS SHALL MAKE.

The first sentence of this clause contains the complete original jurisdiction of the Supreme Court. No other type of case can originate in this court, nor can Congress add to this list. Very few cases start in the Supreme Court. All the other cases that are decided by the high court get there on the basis of its appellate jurisdiction. Congress does have the power to define what this appellate jurisdiction will be. It may increase its jurisdiction, or withdraw certain types of cases from the Supreme Court's appellate jurisdiction. To illustrate how far reaching Congress's power is in this respect, there was the case in 1868 which the Court was in the process of deciding. Before the decision was announced, Congress passed a law withdrawing the Court's jurisdiction in appeals in that particular type of case. The court could do nothing but decide that it did not have jurisdiction; therefore the original case had to be dismissed.

As we have mentioned, the Supreme Court could not possibly hear all the cases that people want it to hear. Actually the Court hears such cases as it feels are important, in addition to the relatively small number it is required to hear by law. Thus if two Courts of Appeals gave conflicting decisions on cases involving the same principle of law, the Supreme Court would take an appeal so as to establish what the law really is. Or if a state court upheld a state law over a federal law, the Supreme Court would have to hear an appeal.

Clause 3. Guarantee of Trial by Jury

THE TRIAL OF ALL CRIMES, EXCEPT IN CASES OF IMPEACHMENT, SHALL BE BY JURY; AND SUCH TRIAL SHALL BE HELD IN THE STATE WHERE THE SAID CRIMES SHALL HAVE BEEN COMMITTED; BUT WHEN NOT COMMITTED WITHIN ANY STATE, THE TRIAL SHALL BE AT SUCH PLACE OR PLACES AS THE CONGRESS MAY BY LAW HAVE DIRECTED.

This clause guarantees a trial by jury to each person accused of a crime by the national government. Further comments on the judicial process are contained under Amendment VI.

Summary of Judicial Power

The federal judicial power may be summarized in the following manner:

Certain types of cases can be heard only in the Supreme Court. In all other instances Congress determines which of the several courts shall exercise jurisdiction. In some cases only federal courts can hear the dispute (like those involving bankruptcy and patent laws); this is exclusive federal jurisdiction. In other areas, Congress has permitted both federal and state courts to hear the dispute. This is called concurrent jurisdiction. Thus, if a citizen of New Jersey sued a citizen of New York for an amount exceeding $50,000 he could bring his suit either in a federal court or a New York state court. In still other areas, Congress has given state courts exclusive jurisdiction. For example, a suit between citizens of different states involving a sum less than $50,000 would be heard originally in a state court.

Except for the very few cases the Supreme Court must hear, the remainder are chosen by the Court by granting a *writ of certiorari* (literally, send the case up). Lawyers file briefs outlining why the Court should hear their case. If four Justices agree to grant the writ, the case is then forwarded from whatever court (state, federal appeals, district, etc.) to the Supreme Court for a hearing.

Section 3   Treason Against the United States

Clause 1. <u>Definition of Treason</u>

> TREASON AGAINST THE UNITED STATES, SHALL CONSIST ONLY IN LEVYING WAR AGAINST THEM, OR IN ADHERING TO THEIR ENEMIES, GIVING THEM AID AND COMFORT. NO PERSON SHALL BE CONVICTED OF TREASON UNLESS ON THE TESTIMONY OF TWO WITNESSES TO THE SAME OVERT ACT, OR ON CONFESSION IN OPEN COURT.

The provisions and terminology of this clause originated in old English laws. This clause narrowly defines treason: levying war against the United States, adhering to our enemies, or giving them aid and comfort. Congress cannot add to this definition. However, Congress can, and has, passed laws that make such activities as sedition, conspiracy, and espionage crimes punishable by long prison sentences or even death.

Notice also that a person cannot be easily convicted of treason. Conviction requires either a public confession or the testimony of at least two witnesses to an overt or public act. One cannot be tried and convicted of treason for merely thinking about, or even planning treasonable activities.

Clause 2. <u>Punishment for Treason</u>

> THE CONGRESS SHALL HAVE POWER TO DECLARE THE PUNISHMENT OF TREASON, BUT NO ATTAINDER OF TREASON SHALL WORK CORRUPTION OF BLOOD OR FORFEITURE EXCEPT DURING THE LIFE OF THE PERSON ATTAINTED.

This is another clause that was important to the framers of the Constitution but it has lost considerable significance for us today. It had been a practice of the English Parliament during the sixteenth and seventeenth centuries to order the confiscation of property belonging to a person guilty of treason. Not only was the accused prohibited from using this property, but through "corruption of blood," his family and heirs could not inherit it from him. Thus one man's crime was visited upon his whole family. This clause limits forfeiture to the duration of a person's life. Several cases arose after the Civil War involving both this clause and the Confiscation Act of 1862.

Article IV

Relations Among the States

Section 1   Full Faith and Credit Clause

FULL FAITH AND CREDIT SHALL BE GIVEN IN EACH STATE TO THE PUBLIC ACTS, RECORDS, AND JUDICIAL PROCEEDINGS OF EVERY OTHER STATE. AND THE CONGRESS MAY BY GENERAL LAWS PRESCRIBE THE MANNER IN WHICH SUCH ACTS, RECORDS, AND PROCEEDINGS SHALL BE PROVED, AND THE EFFECT THEREOF.

This section is known as the full faith and credit clause. It is very important to the people of the United States because it acts to prevent anyone from "beating the law" by moving out of a state before court action may be brought against him.

For example, an Illinois court awards John Doe $1,000,000 in damages against Richard Smith. Smith does not want to pay, so he moves to California. Instead of Doe having to chase Smith to California and bring a new suit in the courts of California, under the full faith and credit clause the California court will honor or recognize the Illinois judgment and enforce it as if it were a California decision.

This clause is also the basis for the validity of a marriage anywhere in the United States. Every state will recognize a marriage legally contracted in another state. Divorce decrees, however, are another matter. These have proved a headache for all the courts, including the Supreme Court. Do all the states have to accept a divorce granted in Nevada? In 1945 the Supreme Court declared "yes," because the petitioner had a *bona fide* domicile in that state. In 1948, to confuse matters, the Court said "no," since any state could determine for itself whether the Nevada courts had jurisdiction or control over the parties. Since these decisions, the Supreme Court has tried to find some "halfway" ground which would give the parties and the states involved a fair share of control over divorce proceedings.

Marriage and divorce are but two relationships that may cause disagreements between citizens of different states. The problem of the courts, under this clause, then becomes one of applying the appropriate law and the trend is to give state courts more leeway.

Section 2   Interstate Citizenship

Clause 1. Privileges and Immunities Clause

> THE CITIZENS OF EACH STATE SHALL BE ENTITLED TO ALL
> PRIVILEGES AND IMMUNITIES OF CITIZENS OF THE SEVERAL STATES.

The clause came into the Constitution directly from the Articles of Confederation. Under the old government, revolutionary leaders had to find some way to reconcile the advantages of a common citizenship (as under the monarchy) with the new concept of state independence. This clause was their answer. It essentially means that a state must not discriminate against out-of-state citizens in favor of its own citizens. A citizen of Kansas, for example, has a right to use Iowa courts, to operate a business there, or to own and dispose of property in Iowa on equal terms with the citizens of Iowa. There are other rights, however, that Iowa may legally deny to citizens of other states, such as the right to participate in elections. Thus, in 1978 the Supreme Court ruled that states may constitutionally require that state policemen be citizens but that an Alaska law giving preference to Alaskan residents in hiring for jobs in that state's oil and gas industries violated this privileges and immunities clause.

Clause 2. Interstate Rendition

A PERSON CHARGED IN ANY STATE WITH TREASON, FELONY,
OR OTHER CRIME, WHO SHALL FLEE FROM JUSTICE, AND BE FOUND
IN ANOTHER STATE, SHALL, ON DEMAND OF THE EXECUTIVE
AUTHORITY OF THE STATE FROM WHICH HE FLED, BE DELIVERED
UP TO BE REMOVED TO THE STATE HAVING JURISDICTION OF THE
CRIME.

This is the basis for what is called "interstate rendition" or "extradition," as it is more commonly called by the newspapers. This clause also presents us with a good example of the way in which the Supreme Court modifies the Constitution. The language is clear and positive. A fugitive found in another state *"shall be delivered up"* upon the demand of the governor of the state wherein the crime was committed. But in applying this principle in actual cases, we find there is no way, short of force, to compel a state to return a fugitive. Rather than involve itself in continual friction and strife, the Supreme Court, in 1860, interpreted the *shall* to mean *may*, therefore changing the meaning from a mandatory command to a moral obligation.

This interpretation has worked well over the years, yet several decisions in the 1980s reflect perhaps the original intent that federal courts could order a state's governor to honor a rendition request.

Clause 3. Fugitive Slaves

NO PERSON HELD TO SERVICE OR LABOR IN ONE STATE, UNDER
THE LAWS THEREOF, ESCAPING INTO ANOTHER, SHALL, IN
CONSEQUENCE OF ANY LAW OR REGULATION THEREIN, BE
DISCHARGED FROM SUCH SERVICE OR LABOR, BUT SHALL BE
DELIVERED UP ON CLAIM OF THE PARTY TO WHOM SUCH SERVICE
OR LABOR MAY BE DUE.

The Thirteenth Amendment abolished slavery and involuntary servitude, making this section obsolete.

Section 3   Admitting New States

Clause 1. <u>Procedure for New States</u>

NEW STATES MAY BE ADMITTED BY THE CONGRESS INTO THIS UNION; BUT NO NEW STATE SHALL BE FORMED OR ERECTED WITHIN THE JURISDICTION OF ANY OTHER STATE; NOR ANY STATE BE FORMED BY THE JUNCTION OF TWO OR MORE STATES, OR PARTS OF STATES, WITHOUT THE CONSENT OF THE LEGISLATURES OF THE STATES CONCERNED AS WELL AS OF THE CONGRESS.

Almost three-fourths of all the states had recourse to this clause at one time or another. Procedures for admitting states have varied through the years but general features have remained the same. The first step is a petition by the inhabitants of a territory to Congress asking for admission. If Congress is favorably disposed it passes an "enabling act" which authorizes the people of the territory to draft a constitution. The final step is approval of the constitution by Congress and the President in what is often called a "statehood bill." The latter is probably the only act of Congress that cannot be repealed.

Territories cannot force Congress to admit them as states. Moreover, they have to accept whatever "conditions" Congress imposes upon them, however onerous they may be. Certain types of conditions, however, are not binding on the government *after* it becomes a state, while other kinds of conditions are binding. An illustration of this point occurred in the case of the capitol of Oklahoma. In 1906, in order to become a state, Oklahoma had to accept a condition of Congress that required it to keep its capitol at Guthrie for seven years. After admittance, Oklahoma changed its capitol to Oklahoma City. The Supreme Court, which eventually heard the dispute, ruled that this was a *political* condition and was not binding. The choice of a capitol city was a political power which all the rest of the states enjoyed. If Oklahoma were deprived of this power, it would not be equal to the other states.

Property conditions are a different matter. The courts treat these conditions as a sort of contractual relationship whose binding character does not lessen a state's political power. For example, New Mexico accepted lands from the United States with the condition that the proceeds would be spent for certain items such as education and highways. Later New Mexico used a portion for publicity purposes. The Supreme Court, in deciding the resultant case, stated that this was a property condition, and therefore binding upon the state.

It was settled by the outcome of the Civil War that no state may withdraw from the Union.

We have five examples in our history of new states being formed from other states: Vermont, Kentucky, Tennessee, Maine, and West Virginia. Permission was readily granted for each case, except West Virginia. This division took place during the Civil War and Virginia's "consent" was achieved only by a wild stretch of the imagination. Interestingly, Texas entered the Union with an agreement with Congress that it could divide itself into as many as five states. Texas has never invoked this privilege.

Clause 2. Acquiring Territory

> THE CONGRESS SHALL HAVE POWER TO DISPOSE OF AND MAKE ALL NEEDFUL RULES AND REGULATIONS RESPECTING THE TERRITORY OR OTHER PROPERTY BELONGING TO THE UNITED STATES; AND NOTHING IN THIS CONSTITUTION SHALL BE SO CONSTRUED AS TO PREJUDICE ANY CLAIMS OF THE UNITED STATES, OR OF ANY PARTICULAR STATE.

This clause, with others, gives Congress complete control over territories. It may legislate directly with respect to the local affairs of a territory, as in Wake Island, or it may delegate that function to a legislature elected by the citizens of the territory, as in Guam. Where Congress delegates this power to the local legislature, this body is limited by the Constitution and the laws of the United States.

Certain territories, only the District of Columbia now, are called *incorporated* territories and are considered integral parts of the United States. All the protections and guarantees of personal liberty found in our Constitution are applicable to the inhabitants of these territories.

The remaining territories, Guam, Samoa, Northern Mariana Islands, Virgin Islands, and trust areas, are *unincorporated* territories. They are not, in a legal sense, considered an integral part of the United States, and only those basic protections of the Constitution (free speech, fair trial, etc.) are applicable, unless Congress provides otherwise. Puerto Rico is called a "commonwealth," and fits constitutionally somewhere between a state and a territory. In accordance with treaty (1978) and legislative (1979) terms, control over the Panama Canal Zone will be shared by the United States and Panamanian governments until the year 2000 when Panama will assume full and complete sovereignty.

Section 4   Guarantee of Republican Form of Government

THE UNITED STATES SHALL GUARANTEE TO EVERY STATE IN THIS UNION A REPUBLICAN FORM OF GOVERNMENT, AND SHALL PROTECT EACH OF THEM AGAINST INVASION; AND, ON APPLICATION OF THE LEGISLATURE, OR OF THE EXECUTIVE (WHEN THE LEGISLATURE CANNOT BE CONVENED), AGAINST DOMESTIC VIOLENCE.

The Constitution does not tell us what is "a republican form of government," nor have the courts been willing to define this phrase in detail. It is widely accepted, however, that the framers had in mind a representative government as distinguished from such forms of government as monarchy or aristocracy.

Whenever cases do come to the courts on this question, the judges usually evade the issue by stating that it is a political question and is to be decided by the political branches of the government—that is, Congress and the President. The fact that a state's Senators and Representatives are seated in Congress is sufficient evidence that it has a "republican form of government."

An invasion of a state, is, of course, an invasion of the United States, and therefore the full weight of our armed forces would be used immediately.

When a state requests assistance, it is usually left to the President to determine whether federal troops will be used to curb "domestic violence." The courts will not interfere with the President's authority under this section because it is another example of a "political question." For example, in 1842 a rebellion occurred in Rhode Island and two governments existed. President John Tyler threatened the use of federal troops on behalf of one of the groups. His action, in effect, determined the legitimate government, and thereafter the courts refused to enter the dispute. The President may send federal troops into a state even over the objection of state officials. This may be done under the President's powers to protect the mails and other U.S. property or to protect interstate commerce or to enforce a federal court decision.

Article V

Method of Amendment

THE CONGRESS, WHENEVER TWO-THIRDS OF BOTH HOUSES SHALL DEEM IT NECESSARY, SHALL PROPOSE AMENDMENTS TO THIS CONSTITUTION, OR, ON THE APPLICATION OF THE LEGISLATURES OF TWO-THIRDS OF THE SEVERAL STATES, SHALL CALL A CONVENTION FOR PROPOSING AMENDMENTS, WHICH IN EITHER CASE SHALL BE VALID, TO ALL INTENTS AND PURPOSES, AS PART OF THIS CONSTITUTION, WHEN RATIFIED BY THE LEGISLATURES OF THREE-FOURTHS OF THE SEVERAL STATES, OR BY CONVENTIONS IN THREE-FOURTHS THEREOF, AS THE ONE OR THE OTHER MODE OF RATIFICATION MAY BE PROPOSED BY THE CONGRESS; <u>PROVIDED THAT NO AMENDMENT WHICH MAY BE MADE PRIOR TO THE YEAR ONE THOUSAND EIGHT HUNDRED AND EIGHT SHALL IN ANY MANNER AFFECT THE FIRST AND FOURTH CLAUSES IN THE NINTH SECTION OF THE FIRST ARTICLE;</u> AND THAT NO STATE, WITHOUT ITS CONSENT, SHALL BE DEPRIVED OF ITS EQUAL SUFFRAGE IN THE SENATE.

The underlined portion of this article referred to the importation of slaves, and therefore has no significance today.

The amending process has two distinct steps: proposing and ratifying. The Congress is involved in the proposal stage whereas the states are involved in the ratifying or approval stage.

There are two methods of proposing amendments: (1) by a two-thirds vote of both houses of Congress, or (2) by a national convention called by Congress at the request of two-thirds of the states. All twenty-seven amendments have been proposed by Congress. Scholarly opinion was that the second method would never be used except for the purpose of overhauling or revising the Constitution completely. However, in recent years campaigns by conservative and religious groups for amendments on voting rights, balanced budgets, and anti-abortion have resulted in many state legislatures passing resolutions (thirty-three in 1969) calling for a convention. No procedure now exists to implement such an event. The two-thirds vote necessary to pass a proposed amendment means two-thirds of the members present. It does *not* mean two-thirds of the full membership. The President does not sign proposed amendments; therefore he cannot veto them.

The second stage of the amending process is ratification. Here again, there are two methods: (1) by three-fourths of the legislatures of the states, or (2) by special constitutional conventions in three-fourths of the states. Congress decides which method is to be used and has specified the legislatures for every amendment except the Twenty-First.

Historical opinion was that once a state had ratified an amendment and notified the federal government, it could not retract its action. In December 1981, a District Court judge in a case involving the Equal Rights Amendment ruled that a state could rescind its previous approval. The Supreme Court, as of this printing, has not rendered a final decision on this issue, but with the amendment's failure of passage, the rescinding question has become moot. However, a previous rejection of a proposed amendment does not bar future favorable action by a state. After the required number of states has ratified, the National Archives and Records Administration, an independent agency in the Executive branch, promulgates the amendment which then becomes a part of our Constitution.

The Congress, in forwarding an amendment to the states, may specify a reasonable time within which they must act. Seven years has been the common limit imposed by Congress. The reason Congress has stipulated a time limit is to prevent proposed amendments from hanging on indefinitely, while conditions and circumstances change. For example, in 1924 Congress submitted a Child Labor Amendment to the states. A number of states acted upon it readily, but never enough to ratify. In the late 1930s congressional legislation was approved by the courts so as to make a child labor amendment unnecessary. Yet in 1937 the Kansas legislature approved of the old proposed amendment. What would happen if the necessary three-fourths of the states did approve of this amendment is hard to say. Complicating matters still further, the Twenty-Seventh Amendment was ratified over a span of 203 years! Another dimension to the time limit was added when Congress extended the seven-year deadline of the proposed Equal Rights Amendment from March 22, 1979, to June 30, 1982. Complicating the issue still further was the same District Court judge who ruled that the Congress could not extend the original time limit. However, the Supreme Court stayed the lower court's ruling when it agreed to hear an appeal on the constitutional issues. Yet the case became moot, since the deadline had expired and the amendment fell three states short of the requisite thirty-eight needed for ratification.

From the first Congress in 1789 until January 1, 1982, over 7,000 amendments have been introduced in Congress. However, only thirty-four including the famous Bill of Rights, received congressional approval and were submitted to the states. Of these thirty-four, twenty-seven have been ratified and six are considered legally dead and one could be considered pending.

The last clause of this article dealing with senatorial representation is considered by most constitutional lawyers to be the only part of the Constitution that cannot be amended. Naturally, no state would consent to giving up its equal representation in the Senate.

Article VI

Supremacy of United States Law

Clause 1. The Public Debt

ALL DEBTS CONTRACTED AND ENGAGEMENTS ENTERED INTO, BEFORE THE ADOPTION OF THIS CONSTITUTION, SHALL BE AS VALID AGAINST THE UNITED STATES UNDER THIS CONSTITUTION AS UNDER THE CONFEDERATION.

You will recall from our earlier discussion on the making of the Constitution that the financial conditions of the Confederation, as well as the individual states, were precarious. Currencies and securities issued by the several governments had declined so much that they were practically worthless. A number of citizens had loaned money to the several state governments during and after the Revolutionary War and the Confederation had borrowed large sums from foreign governments and foreign citizens. In all, the Confederation and the states owed over $79,000,000 to domestic and foreign creditors.

If we repudiated or reneged on our debts, then our credit standing throughout the world, as well as at home, would have been valueless. Thus, this section announced to one and all that the new government would stand behind the old debts contracted by the Confederation. Later, Alexander Hamilton, the Secretary of the Treasury in Washington's cabinet, persuaded Congress to take over the debts that had been incurred by the individual states in the war. Needless to say, the United States did pay off these debts quickly and at their face value.

Clause 2. Hierarchy of Law in the United States

THIS CONSTITUTION, AND THE LAWS OF THE UNITED STATES WHICH SHALL BE MADE IN PURSUANCE THEREOF, AND ALL TREATIES MADE, OR WHICH SHALL BE MADE, UNDER THE AUTHORITY OF THE UNITED STATES, SHALL BE THE SUPREME LAW OF THE LAND; AND THE JUDGES IN EVERY STATE SHALL BE BOUND THEREBY,

ANYTHING IN THE CONSTITUTION OR LAWS OR ANY STATE TO THE
CONTRARY NOTWITHSTANDING.

The Constitution is the supreme or highest law in the United
States. All other law, national or state, which is in conflict with any
part of the Constitution must be null and void. Furthermore, any law
passed by Congress, or any treaty entered into by the United States,
provided it is not in conflict with the Constitution, is superior to the
constitutions or laws of the states. There is one national law system,
uniform and applicable throughout the United States.

Of course, Congress cannot legislate on every activity because,
as we have pointed out, the federal government has only those powers
enumerated or implied from the Constitution. But whenever it
legislates or acts within its powers, the federal law is supreme and
state courts have to recognize that supremacy. Here, then, we see
more evidence of the principle of federalism at work. Powers have
been divided between the governments, and the task of the Supreme
Court is to ascertain whether a challenged state law or national statute
has been rightfully exercised. For example, Arizona challenged the
construction of the Hoover (Boulder) Dam because the plans of the
project had not been submitted to its state engineer as required by
Arizona law. The Supreme Court, applying the supremacy clause,
among others, stated that, "if Congress has power to authorize the
construction of the dam and reservoir, Wilbur (Secretary of the
Interior) is under no obligation to submit the plans and specifications
to the State Engineer for approval."

Another example wherein a treaty superseded state laws occurred
in the famous migratory bird case in 1920. The Supreme Court ruled
that when the United States and Great Britain signed a treaty for the
protection of birds flying between the United States and Canada, the
national law replaced all state laws in this area.

State court judges are specifically required to apply and enforce
the national Constitution and national laws in cases in which there is
a conflict between national and state statutes or constitutions.
Sometimes state courts uphold their own laws as against national
statutes. But in such cases the Supreme Court of the United States

may review and reverse the state court decision.

Clause 3. <u>Oath of Allegiance</u>

> THE SENATORS AND REPRESENTATIVES BEFORE MENTIONED, AND THE MEMBERS OF THE SEVERAL STATE LEGISLATURES, AND ALL EXECUTIVE AND JUDICIAL OFFICERS, BOTH OF THE UNITED STATE AND OF THE SEVERAL STATES, SHALL BE BOUND BY OATH OR AFFIRMATION TO SUPPORT THIS CONSTITUTION; BUT NO RELIGIOUS TEST SHALL EVER BE REQUIRED AS A QUALIFICATION TO ANY OFFICE OR PUBLIC TRUST UNDER THE UNITED STATES.

All officers, state as well as federal, are bound to support the United States Constitution. The first oath prescribed by Congress was a simple affirmation of support. Later, in times of crisis, the spirit of the oath was changed to include a positive assertion of loyalty to not only the Constitution, but to our laws, treaties, and institutions as well. In the post-World War II period, amid the cold war atmosphere, loyalty and security loomed as significant aspects of this clause.

By this section state officers and state agencies may be intrusted with certain federal duties and functions. For example, the selective service, or military draft, process is a joint undertaking by federal and state officials.

The prohibition on religious tests or qualifications for federal officials is another example of the democratic and tolerant philosophy of the framers. Such religious tests were quite common in several of the colonies and even extended over into the republic period insofar as state officers were concerned. Although the religious clause is not a prohibition on the states, almost all the states have similar provisions in their constitutions.

Article VII

Ratification of the Constitution

> THE RATIFICATION OF THE CONVENTIONS OF NINE STATES SHALL BE SUFFICIENT FOR THE ESTABLISHMENT OF THIS CONSTITUTION BETWEEN THE STATES SO RATIFYING THE SAME.

This article has only historical interest for us today. It provided a method of putting the new Constitution into effect. Technically, the Constitutional Convention had no authority to construct a new instrument of government. Nor could it assume that this document was an amendment to the old Articles of Confederation. Furthermore, the Articles required the unanimous consent of all the states before an amendment could become effective. The new Constitution, however, required the consent of only nine states, a decidedly unconstitutional procedure. The fact that the Constitution was ratified by nine states, that new officers were chosen, that the new government did function and that it was accepted by the people, makes all discussion about its legality pure speculation.

Chapter 5

The Amendments

In 204 years only twenty-seven amendments have been added to the original Constitution. This is a marvelous record and one of which the people of the United States should be justly proud. It illustrates not only the wisdom of the framers, but also the understanding and good sense of generations of American citizens.

The first ten amendments are often considered part of the original Constitution because they were enacted so soon after the government began to operate. Also their proposal stemmed directly from criticisms voiced during the ratification struggle. In 1789 the Federalist party leaders, true to their promises, proposed twelve amendments which would protect individuals from interference or oppression by the national government. The states approved ten amendments and they became a part of our Constitution, forever known as the *Bill of Rights*. Our basic liberties and guarantees from oppression are contained in these ten amendments.

Within a few years after the adoption of the Bill of Rights, the Eleventh and Twelfth Amendments were added. Then followed a long period of inaction until the three Civil War amendments were ratified between 1865 and 1870. Nearly half a century passed before a flurry of four amendments occurred between 1913 and 1920. In 1933 the Twentieth and Twenty-First Amendments took effect. The Twenty-Second Amendment became law in 1951; the Twenty-Third in 1961; the Twenty-Fourth in 1964; the Twenty-Fifth in 1967; and the Twenty-Sixth in 1971; and finally, the Twenty-Seventh in May, 1992, though it was actually proposed in 1789.

In the following pages some of the background and reasons for each amendment are presented in addition to a detailed discussion of the meaning of the words and phrases.

Amendment 1

Proposed September 25, 1789   Ratified December 15, 1791

Freedom of Religion, Speech, Press, Assembly, and Petition

<u>Freedom of Religion</u>

> CONGRESS SHALL MAKE NO LAW RESPECTING AN ESTABLISHMENT OF RELIGION, OR PROHIBITING THE FREE EXERCISE THEREOF;

In the early decades of our history the First Amendment was considered as applying only against actions by the national government. Since the 1920s, however, the courts have stated that the protections of the First Amendment are included in the Fourteenth Amendment and apply to state and local governments as well.

The First Amendment should not be interpreted to make us think that the founding fathers were antireligious. The truth is that they were, by and large, deeply religious men. However, they did not want to see the establishment of an official religion for the whole United States (as the Anglican Church is the official religion in England). The First Amendment not only bans the creation of a national religion but also prevents the national and state governments from favoring one religion over another. Neither government can pass laws that aid one church or discriminate against another. Nor can the governments force persons to join a church or stay away from a church. No tax may be levied by either government for the support of any church or its activities. And it goes almost without saying that the national or state governments cannot participate in the affairs of any religious organization.

The Constitution, we should emphasize, does not make our

governments antireligious. There are a number of things that either government may do without violating the First Amendment. For example, public funds may be used to furnish nonsectarian textbooks to parochial schools and to provide transportation for parochial students. Surplus agricultural products may be obtained by religious schools for lunch programs under the same conditions as public schools. Churches have been traditionally exempt from general property taxes. Public schools may release students for the purpose of obtaining religious instruction in buildings not under the control of public authorities. However, public schools may not compel the reading of a prayer in classrooms, even though several states would like to see such a policy adopted and have supported a proposed constitutional amendment toward that end. New dimensions are constantly added; for example, in January, 1982, a lower federal court ruled that "creationism" is a "religion" and therefore an Arkansas law requiring its teaching in public schools violated the First Amendment.

This section also protects a person's freedom to believe and to practice religious doctrine, no matter how odd or different from the traditional ideas of religion. However, religious belief cannot be used as a justification for certain acts which the government has declared, by law, to be crimes. For example, the belief in and practice of polygamy cannot be defended in the United States on the ground of religious freedom. Congress has declared such a practice a crime. Nor can freedom of religion protect a person who violently abuses a police officer. Thus, while the free exercise of religion is permitted, it does not mean that everything which may be called "religion" may be tolerated. Conversely, states may not force children of Jehovah's Witnesses to salute the flag at school, or impose unreasonable rules on religious groups when soliciting door-to-door, or deny meeting space to religious sects at state-owned universities. Thus, in 1990, the Court ruled that the drug peyote, considered essential and sacred by some Indian tribes, can be regulated under a state's general drug laws; yet conversely, the Court ruled, unanimously, in 1993 that religious groups have a constitutional right to sacrifice animals during worship.

Freedom of Speech and Press

OR ABRIDGING THE FREEDOM OF SPEECH, OR OF PRESS;

Democracy, as we know and practice it in these United States, is founded on the belief in the free exchange of ideas and information. A free and uncensored press is a democratic press. The right to speak one's mind is also inherent in a democratic system. However, we should remember that a person cannot say or print anything he wants. Freedom of speech and press is not absolute because such unlimited action might injure another person. Thus libelous statements (written defamation) and slanderous statements (oral defamation) may be punishable by either the injured party, by the government, or by both injured party and government. Also, freedom of speech and press may be restricted when there is a "clear and present danger" to the security of the nation. Thus statements that might obstruct the recruitment of military personnel or cause insubordination in the armed services when the United States is at war would not be protected by this amendment. The danger in this instance would be real and immediate. At other times, these same statements would not cause trouble and so would be permitted. The "clear and present danger" doctrine, as this is called, is applied to specific cases. The idea is somewhat similar to the action of a person yelling "Fire" in a crowded theater. Untold damage could be done to individuals and property if the crowd stampeded. However, if the theater were empty when a person yelled "Fire," there would be little cause for alarm.

Similarly, inflammatory and "fighting words" may be restricted or punished. Courts have denied absolute constitutional protection to words inciting others to violence or utterances that, by their very nature, may provoke their victims to use physical force. Conversely, the Court ruled in 1993 that people who commit "hate crimes" motivated by bigotry, may be given longer sentences and not violate the free speech clause of the Constitution.

A 1972 ruling of the Supreme Court has somewhat limited freedom of the press by holding that the First Amendment does not give a newspaper reporter the right to refuse to testify before grand juries or other investigative bodies as to the sources of his information. Several states have passed so-called shield laws granting reporters this exemption, but the federal government has not acted though Congress did pass the Freedom of Information Act providing access to almost all government material. On the other hand, when in 1971 the federal government sought to prohibit the *New York Times* from publishing the so-called Pentagon Papers, the Supreme Court ruled that such a prohibition would be a violation of freedom of the press.

Our courts have been extremely reluctant to approve laws that require a person to obtain permission or a license in order to publish or speak. Laws imposing prior restraint or prior censorship are always considered suspect by the Court. In a few areas, a certain amount of censorship is permitted (if carefully regulated). For example, the national government regulates the radio and television industry because there is only a limited number of frequency bands on which to broadcast (unlike the newspaper and magazine industry, where there are no such natural limitations). A certain amount of regulation is allowed in licensing sound trucks, which blare forth in parks and on the streets. The courts have ruled that picketing in strikes is protected by the First Amendment, as long as it remains *peaceful.*

In recent years the question of obscene literature, art, and movies has preoccupied the people and courts of the United States. Although obscenity, as such, has never been protected by the First Amendment, and the states may enact some regulatory laws, in the past there was no universally accepted legal definition of obscenity. During the 1960s the Warren Court promulgated a series of tests that led to extensive litigation. In 1973, by a close vote, the Burger Court set down new guidelines. States may now ban any works that (1) taken as a whole, appeal to prurient interests; (2) portray sexual conduct in a patently offensive way; (3) taken as a whole, do not have serious literary, artistic, political, or scientific value. Local community standards rather than national attitudes are to be used to judge such works. As anticipated these guidelines generated still more court cases.

The courts are continually faced with the problem of weighing the rights of an individual or a business against the rights of the whole society. Our rights, as well as our duties and responsibilities, depend upon how the courts decide each specific case.

Right of Assembly and Petition

> OR THE RIGHT OF THE PEOPLE PEACEABLY TO ASSEMBLE,
> AND TO PETITION THE GOVERNMENT FOR A REDRESS OF
> GRIEVANCES.

This clause protects the right of persons to gather together in public meetings. This is fundamental to our democratic society where we depend so much upon our political parties and clubs, and our social, religious, and economic organizations. As long as the meeting is orderly, no matter who the sponsors or speakers are, the First Amendment (and the Fourteenth) protects the assembly. Bear in mind again, that this right, like our other civil liberties, is relative and not absolute. Unreasonable actions by a group or by an individual cannot be protected by this clause (such as a sit-in or students taking over a college president's office). Thus, a public demonstration, held without authority, on a busy street corner would disrupt the community unreasonably. The arbitrary refusal by a public official of a union's request for a permit to hold an orderly public meeting in a park or public building would violate this clause, as would applying the same law unfairly or irregularly to different groups.

The right of petition can be traced as far back as the Magna Carta of 1215. This clause guarantees our right to communicate with those who operate our governments. It does not mean that government officials have to act on these petitions; but public opinion has a great influence over the actions of our legislators and executives. Furthermore, a number of groups—farmers, business, labor, professional, and reform—have paid agents, called *lobbyists*, at the capitols to look after the interests of their groups. They keep the legislators and administrators informed on the attitudes and desires of their members.

New emphasis has been given to this section by recent Supreme Court decisions interpreting the Federal Election Campaign Act and various state and local political practices. The Court has ruled that this clause protects an individual's freedom to associate with whatever political party he or she wishes and that political firings are illegal; minor parties do not have to disclose contributors; citizens cannot be limited in funds they want to contribute to groups supporting local issues, but the federal government can restrict the political activity of federal workers.

Amendment 2

Proposed September 25, 1789   Ratified December 15, 1791

Right to Keep and Bear Arms

A WELL REGULATED MILITIA BEING NECESSARY TO THE SECURITY OF A FREE STATE, THE RIGHT OF THE PEOPLE TO KEEP AND BEAR ARMS SHALL NOT BE INFRINGED.

This is another protection against a possible abuse by Congress. The right protected is really the right of a state to maintain an armed militia, or national guard, as we call it now. In the eighteenth century people feared that Congress might, by passing a law, prohibit the states from arming their citizens. Then, having all the armed strength at its command, the national government could overwhelm the states. Such a circumstance has never happened, but this amendment would prevent it. The Second Amendment does not give anybody or everybody the right to possess and use firearms. The states may very properly prescribe regulations and permits governing the use of guns within their borders. Moreover, this amendment does not bar Congress from passing a law regulating the sale and distribution of shotguns less than eighteen inches in length. This law was passed in 1934 to counteract gangsterism rampant at that time.

Federal regulation of firearms is a hotly contested issue, with the so-called Brady Bill having been vetoed by President Bush but signed by President Clinton in 1993. This amendment applies only to the national government. States may pass as restrictive gun control legislation as possible without violating the Second Amendment.

Amendment 3

Proposed September 25, 1789   Ratified December 15, 1791

No Quartering of Soldiers

NO SOLDIER SHALL IN TIME OF PEACE BE QUARTERED IN ANY HOUSE WITHOUT THE CONSENT OF THE OWNER, NOR IN TIME OF WAR, BUT IN A MANNER TO BE PRESCRIBED BY LAW.

The origin of this amendment may be traced to the difficulties between the colonists and the British authorities immediately before the Revolutionary War. In several of the cities, English troops were stationed or lodged in private homes without the consent of the owners. Naturally the colonists resented these invasions of their privacy. In the debates over the ratification of the Constitution and on the proposed amendments, the people seemed to think this amendment was necessary. The language and the meaning of the amendment are clear. During peacetime, the national government cannot place a soldier in a private home to live without the owner's permission. In time of war this may be done, but only under conditions set down in a law passed by Congress.

Amendment 4

Proposed September 25, 1789   Ratified December 15, 1791

Unreasonable Search and Seizures

THE RIGHT OF THE PEOPLE TO BE SECURE IN THEIR PERSONS, HOUSES, PAPERS, AND EFFECTS, AGAINST UNREASONABLE SEARCHES AND SEIZURES, SHALL NOT BE VIOLATED, AND NO WARRANTS SHALL ISSUE, BUT UPON PROBABLE CAUSE, SUPPORTED BY OATH OR AFFIRMATION, AND PARTICULARLY DESCRIBING THE PLACE TO BE SEARCHED, AND THE PERSONS OR THINGS TO BE SEIZED.

The Fourth Amendment offers protection not only against physical searches, but also against a search of a person's house, place of business, personal and business papers, and even his garage and vehicle. But remember, only *unreasonable* searches and seizures are forbidden. Reasonable searches are permitted under certain conditions. First a warrant (an order from a judicial officer) must be obtained. The warrant must state the thing to be searched and the thing to be seized. A belief, no matter how well founded, that an article associated with a crime is hidden in a house, does not give a police officer the right to search without first getting a warrant. However, the officers may search a person, even without a warrant, in connection with the immediate arrest of that person. Police officers may even search the immediate area where they have made the arrest.

The courts have permitted police officers greater leeway for their searches in cases where artificial persons (corporations, trusts) are involved. Also the courts have recognized that modern means of transportation have made the job of law enforcement more difficult. The courts will allow police officers to search airplanes, ships, and automobiles and seize contraband without a warrant because contraband could be moved out of the locality before a warrant could be obtained.

With the advent of wiretaps and electronic listening devices, which can invade the privacy of a person's conversations, a new dimension has been added to the protections of the Fourth Amendment. In 1928, the Supreme Court ruled that wiretapping was not unconstitutional. In 1967, the Court reversed itself and declared such interceptions of conversations a violation of the Fourth Amendment. In 1968, Congress passed the Crime Control Act, permitting state and federal police to tap telephones provided that they received proper judicial authorization. The Act also permitted the President, in cases involving national security, to authorize wiretaps without prior judicial approval. In 1972, however, when a case on wiretapping by federal officials, who acted without prior judicial authorization on a domestic matter, came to the Supreme Court, the justices held the action illegal. The question of the

President's inherent powers to order actions (like wiretapping, burglary, and breaking and entering) that in different circumstances might be considered crimes was one of the significant points raised in the Watergate investigations.

The protections given by this amendment are closely related to the provisions against self-incrimination found in the Fifth Amendment. The national government cannot use evidence illegally seized. Otherwise, this illegal evidence might lead to a conviction. No matter how justified it was, two wrongs do not make a right. A Supreme Court decision in 1960 also extends the ban in federal courts to evidence illegally seized by state officials or private persons. Finally in 1961, this prohibition was extended, under the Fourteenth Amendment, to state courts.

Amendment 5

Proposed September 25, 1789   Ratified December 15, 1791

Rights of Persons in Criminal and Civil Matters

<u>Indictment by Grand Jury</u>

> NO PERSON SHALL BE HELD TO ANSWER FOR A CAPITAL OR OTHERWISE INFAMOUS CRIME, UNLESS ON A PRESENTMENT OR INDICTMENT OF A GRAND JURY, EXCEPT IN CASES ARISING IN THE LAND OR NAVAL FORCES, OR IN THE MILITIA, WHEN IN ACTUAL SERVICE IN TIME OF WAR OR PUBLIC DANGER;

The *grand jury* is another old English institution. The grand jury is composed of twelve to twenty-three persons (usually twenty-three) who have been selected from the district. The grand jury is concerned with the more serious violations of the law, such as murder, espionage, tax evasion, counterfeiting, and the like. The grand jury listens to and analyzes evidence connected with a crime claimed to have been committed by some individual. If the grand jury decides that there is sufficient evidence to warrant a trial, it *indicts*, or formally accuses, the person. If it decides that the evidence is not sufficient to hold a trial, it brings in what is called a *no bill*—refuses to indict.

A *presentment* and *indictment* are essentially the same. If the grand jury has collected evidence itself and then accuses, it is called a presentment. If its decision is based on evidences submitted by the prosecuting officer (the usual case), it is called an indictment. Grand jury proceedings are secret and one-sided, taking up only what the prosecutor wants to bring before the jurors. A majority vote is all that is necessary to bring in an indictment. The grand jury does *not* determine the guilt or innocence of an individual; the trial jury does.

Notice that military personnel are excluded from grand jury proceedings. They have their own court martial system. Militia or national guard personnel are subject to military courts *only* when they are on active duty during wartime or extreme danger. Otherwise, they are civilians and have full rights to grand jury protection. Civilians, even when working for the armed services, are protected by this amendment, as are the civilian dependents of military personnel.

Indictment by grand jury has not been included within the protections of the Fourteenth Amendment. Therefore, states may use other methods to accuse persons of crimes.

No Double Jeopardy

NOR SHALL ANY PERSON BE SUBJECT FOR THE SAME OFFENSE TO BE TWICE PUT IN JEOPARDY OF LIFE OR LIMB;

In the legal sense, jeopardy means the danger an accused person undergoes when he or she is put on trial for a criminal offense. This clause prevents the placing of an accused's life (or liberty) in danger more than once for the same offense. We call it *double jeopardy.* Thus a convicted mail robber could not be tried again for the same robbery.

It might happen that a single action on the part of a criminal would result in several "offenses." He may be tried separately for each "offense." However, if he could show that the same evidence is needed to convict him for all the charges, then this clause would ban any prosecution beyond the first conviction. If a trial is discontinued before a verdict is reached, then the circumstances in each case would determine if the accused could be tried again. For example, a "hung jury" (one that cannot agree on a verdict) would not bar a new trial.

It also might happen that a single offense would violate both federal and state laws (kidnapping, for example). Either or both governments could try the accused. A conviction in the state court would not bar further prosecution by the federal government because two different governments are involved. If a person is acquitted (pronounced not guilty) in a lower federal court, the government is prevented by this clause from appealing the decision to a higher court, though prosecutors could appeal a sentence they considered too lenient. Of course, if the accused is found guilty, he may appeal to a higher court. In 1981, the court ruled, that a state cannot have a second chance to try to convince a jury to impose the death penalty on a convicted person.

No Self-Incrimination

NOR SHALL BE COMPELLED IN ANY CRIMINAL CASE TO BE A
WITNESS AGAINST HIMSELF;

This clause is often referred to as the *freedom from self-incrimination* clause. A witness in any proceeding where testimony is legally required (in a court, committee of Congress, regulatory agency, etc.) may refuse to answer any question *provided:* that his answer might be used for later criminal prosecution or used to uncover further evidence against him. Thus if a suspected bribe-taker were asked: "Did you accept bribes?" he may refuse to answer on the ground this answer would incriminate him. For if he said "yes," he would admit guilt; if he said "no," he would be open for perjury charges.

This clause affords protection only for a witness and only where criminal matters are concerned. A witness would have to answer embarrassing and insulting questions about his own character or any other person. In a criminal trial, if the defendant takes the stand on his own behalf, he may be cross-examined on all matters. Then, too, if the government grants a person an "immunity" (freedom from prosecution) for his testimony, or if the person could no longer be prosecuted for the offense, he *must* testify, because he could not, under these circumstances, incriminate himself. Plea bargaining, a procedure whereby a defendant pleads guilty to one or lesser charges while the prosecutor drops other or more serious charges (thus resulting in quicker trials and lesser penalties) has been given constitutional sanction.

Recent Court decisions apply the freedom from self-incrimination to state and local jurisdictions. Moreover, the protection extends to persons being questioned by police. Thus, under the *Miranda* decision, a person must be advised of his rights—to remain silent, to have an attorney present, to know that his testimony may be used against him—before he may be interrogated. Otherwise, information obtained from him cannot be used in court.

Due Process of Law

NOR BE DEPRIVED OF LIFE, LIBERTY, OR PROPERTY, WITHOUT
DUE PROCESS OF LAW;

This is a short, but very important clause. Probably more cases have been taken to the Supreme Court on the basis of the *due process of law clause* than on any other section in our Constitution. Actually there are two such clauses. This one, in the Fifth Amendment, applies against the national government. A similar clause in the Fourteenth Amendment applies against state governments. The origins of these phrases can be traced as far back as 1215 in the Magna Carta. Despite its ancient origin, we still have no exact definition of the term. Our courts have repeatedly said that its meaning will be found in each specific case. That is, no general rule has been announced which will satisfy all cases. Nevertheless, we do know something about the phrase—it can be classified as either procedural or substantive.

Procedural due process of law is the older meaning. We generally associate it with the procedures or ways of executing our laws. Procedural due process requires a hearing before a judgment or sentence is imposed. The hearing should be as fair and impartial as circumstances permit. We generally think of procedural due process in connection with our regular judicial process, whether it be before a regular court or an administrative agency. For example, Mr. A petitions the Federal Communications Commission for a license to operate a TV station. The Commission, without giving A a chance to present evidence to support his petition, arbitrarily denies him the license. In such a case, the courts would probably declare that the Commission's action was lacking in due process of law.

Substantive due process of law is a newer idea, developing in the United States after the 1890s. Substantive due process deals with the content, the purposes of a law, as well as its procedural arrangements. Substantive due process challenges the wisdom of the law—it acts to determine whether a law is reasonable (due), just, or fair. Substantive due process acts on all branches of the government. For example, let us assume our friend Mr. A receives his permit for a TV station, but the FCC requires that he telecast only between the hours of 7 A.M. and 3 P.M. Again our courts would probably declare the commission's action as lacking in due process, this time, because such conditions would be unreasonable or unfair and not because he was denied a hearing.

Notice that this clause (and the one in the Fourteenth Amendment) protects "life, liberty, and property" of "persons." By "persons" we include aliens and corporations as well as citizens. Protection of life and property are well understood. The courts have interpreted "liberty" to mean "liberty of contract." That is, the liberty of an employee to contract with an employer for services. By interpreting the clause in this manner, the courts declared a number of laws dealing with the regulation of economic enterprises unconstitutional. For almost half a century substantive due process of law and liberty of contract went hand in hand. However, in the late 1930s the Supreme Court began to withdraw from the area of economic regulation. At the same time, the Court began to pay more attention to the content of laws that affected our civil liberties, such as free speech, press, and religion.

Constitutional argumentation and courtroom niceties notwithstanding, the fleshing out of substantive due process of law in contemporary society is a bitter experience. For example, from the *Roe v. Wade* decision of 1973, battles between Pro-Choice and Pro-Life advocates, Straights and Gays over abortion, contraception, life styles, etc., have fluctuated between the rhetoric of the courtroom and the violence of the street and have run the gamut from singing slogans, demonstrations, and blockades to murder!

Just Compensation

NOR SHALL PRIVATE PROPERTY BE TAKEN FOR PUBLIC USE, WITHOUT JUST COMPENSATION.

The power to take private property for public purposes is called the right of *eminent domain*. Every government has such a power. The property taken by the government must be for a public purpose. The courts, however, have upheld the taking of private property for such purposes as parks, national forests, or memorials, as well as for government buildings, military posts, and the like. The state or local governments may not interfere with the national government's power of eminent domain—not even if the property is owned and being used by these governments.

Notice that the government cannot confiscate private property outright. The owner is entitled to "just compensation," which is essentially the market value of the property taken. For example, Mr. Z owns the building and land on the corner of Main and Broad streets. The government wants to build a new post office there. Mr. Z rejects the government's offer to sell his land and building, so the government uses its power of eminent domain. It condemns the property (through court proceedings) and awards Mr. Z a sum of money equal to what he would have received if he had sold it to another person; that is, the market value of the property.

Sometimes it is not necessary that the government physically take possession of private property in order to invoke this protection. For example, the constant noise and glare of military planes at an airport interfered with the normal use of adjoining land as a chicken farm, and the owner was awarded compensation. However, the fact that a governmental action interferes with the conduct of a person's business does not mean that compensation must always be paid. During World War II, the government took over the entire output of a steel manufacturer, and although the manufacturer could not fulfill his orders to other manufacturers, he was still not entitled to further compensation.

Amendment 6

Proposed September 25, 1789   Ratified December 15, 1791

Rights of Accused in Federal Criminal Proceedings

IN ALL CRIMINAL PROSECUTIONS, THE ACCUSED SHALL ENJOY THE RIGHT TO A SPEEDY AND PUBLIC TRIAL, BY AN IMPARTIAL JURY OF THE STATE AND DISTRICT WHEREIN THE CRIME SHALL HAVE BEEN COMMITTED, WHICH DISTRICT SHALL HAVE BEEN PREVIOUSLY ASCERTAINED BY LAW, AND TO BE INFORMED OF THE NATURE AND CAUSE OF THE ACCUSATION; TO BE CONFRONTED WITH THE WITNESSES AGAINST HIM; TO HAVE COMPULSORY PROCESS FOR OBTAINING WITNESSES IN HIS FAVOR, AND TO HAVE THE ASSISTANCE OF COUNSEL FOR HIS DEFENSE.

This amendment is very important because it establishes the standards of procedure to be used in federal courts in criminal cases. Many of the points mentioned here came directly from English court practice as modified by the colonies and states.

A trial should not be so *speedy* as to arrest a person today, indict him tomorrow, and convict him on the third day. That is too speedy. On the other hand, an accused should not be made to wait months or years with a charge hanging over his head. A speedy trial would be one where both the prosecution and defense have had a reasonable time to prepare their cases. Congress established one hundred days between arrest and trial as the standard; many states use 180 days.

A *public trial* is one where the press and general public may attend. This amendment prohibits "star chamber" or secret trials (common to totalitarian countries) where a person may be "railroaded" to prison without even his family knowing about it. Certain trials, however, may result in the disclosure of security secrets or the testimony may be of an obscene nature. The presiding judge could exclude the general public, and possibly the press, while this information is being given.

Courts have been wrestling with the problems posed by the potential conflict of First Amendment (free speech and press) and Sixth Amendment (fair, public trial) so as to protect the rights of all parties. In 1979 the Supreme Court ruled that the guarantee of a public trial assures the right of the defendant, not the press or the public, in a pretrial hearing. In 1980 it ruled that the First Amendment guarantees citizens and members of the press the right to attend criminal trials, though the judge may set some limits.

An *impartial jury* is required for a fair hearing. It usually means that anyone having an interest in the case, such as relatives, business associates, friends, enemies, or persons with very strong prejudices in the matter, should not be on the jury. An accused certainly would not want a personal friend of the prosecutor on the jury. Neither would the prosecutor want a cousin of the accused. In recent years, an impartial jury has also meant an end to the systematic exclusion of African-Americans, women, poor persons, etc., from juries. A federal jury consists of twelve persons and *all* must agree on a verdict, whereas in state courts a jury of fewer than twelve is permitted and a decision may be rendered by less than a unanimous jury. A jury of six, the Court has said, must reach its verdict unanimously. An accused person may waive a jury if the government consents and the court approves. The trial must take place in the locality or district where the offense is charged to have been committed. Under certain circumstances the accused may request that the trial be held in a different district.

An accused person must be *informed of the charges* that the government is preferring against him. Then he can make adequate preparation for his defense before the trial begin. He or his lawyer must be given an opportunity at the trial to *question* or *confront witnesses* who testify against him. Also the court can order persons into court to *testify on behalf of the accused*, if he so requests.

This amendment guarantees an accused person the *right to counsel*. That is, if he cannot hire his own lawyer, the court must provide him with legal assistance at all stages of the criminal proceedings (so-called Miranda rights). Even if several persons are charged with the same crime, a separate lawyer could be demanded by each. An accused may waive this right to counsel, provided he understands what he is doing, but the courts are reluctant to approve of a waiver.

Through the Fourteenth Amendment the right to counsel also operates with regard to state criminal proceedings. Moreover, in a 1972 decision the Supreme Court extended the right to include practically all types of crimes rather than just the more serious crimes as had been the practice.

Amendment 7

Proposed September 25, 1789   Ratified December 15, 1791

Jury Trial in Civil Cases

IN SUITS AT COMMON LAW, WHERE THE VALUE IN CONTROVERSY SHALL EXCEED TWENTY DOLLARS, THE RIGHT OF TRIAL BY JURY SHALL BE PRESERVED, AND NO FACT TRIED BY A JURY SHALL BE OTHERWISE REEXAMINED IN ANY COURT OF THE UNITED STATES, THAN ACCORDING TO THE RULES OF THE COMMON LAW.

This amendment requires a jury trial in federal courts in cases involving twenty or more dollars. "Trial by jury" means a trial by a jury of twelve persons in a court presided over by a judge who has the power to instruct the jury on the law and advise them on the facts. That is to say, the jury decides questions of fact—did car A hit car B? The judge decides questions of law—is this dented fender admissible as evidence?

The requirement of a trial by jury applies only to courts under the jurisdiction of the U.S. government and not to state courts. It applies to common law and to suits arising out of statutory law (that is, to restrain an action by some administrative agency), but it does not apply to suits at equity (that is, where a person seeks remedial protection, such as an injunction). Also, it is possible for the parties to a dispute to waive a jury trial and permit the judge to hear and decide the case. Recent cases have permitted a jury of fewer than twelve, though it is still unsettled as to exactly how many are required for a verdict.

Amendment 8

Proposed September 25, 1789   Ratified December 15, 1791

No Excessive Bail or Unusual Punishment

EXCESSIVE BAIL SHALL NOT BE REQUIRED, NOR EXCESSIVE FINES IMPOSED, NOR CRUEL AND UNUSUAL PUNISHMENTS INFLICTED.

The words "excessive," "cruel," and "unusual" in this Amendment are so vague and general that their exact meaning has been left to the courts to decide. What an excessive bail or fine is depends upon a number of things, such as: the seriousness of the crime, the reputation or record of the offender, and whether he is able to pay. For example, bail of $100,000 for a person who has robbed a store is entirely out of order. On the other hand, a large bail on a person who has repeatedly been in trouble with the police would be more in order. Bail is not usually allowed for persons facing trial for murder or other major crime.

Cruel and unusual punishment mainly refers to the use of torture, though there again the court has the final say. The penalty of a long term in prison for a relatively minor offense, e.g., making a false statement in a public record, would be cruel and unusual punishment within the meaning of this amendment. Up until 1972 the death penalty had not been considered a cruel and unusual punishment, whether inflicted by electrocution, hanging, lethal gas, or a firing squad. In a close 5–4 decision, the Supreme Court that year held that the death penalty is a cruel and unusual punishment because of the inadequacies and inequities in our legal system. Subsequent decisions have spelled out further considerations (only in cases of murder, only after mitigating circumstances have been taken into account, automatic appeals for those alleged to be insane at time of crime; due consideration to effects of child abuse or mental retardation, etc.) on when and how the death penalty may be imposed.

Amendment 9

Proposed September 25, 1789   Ratified December 15, 1791

Rights Retained by the People

THE ENUMERATION IN THE CONSTITUTION OF CERTAIN RIGHTS SHALL NOT BE CONSTRUED TO DENY OR DISPARAGE OTHERS RETAINED BY THE PEOPLE.

This is a difficult amendment to understand. In order to get at its meaning you will have to recall the philosophy and state of mind of the colonists during the Revolutionary period. Many Americans, following the philosophy of John Locke, believed that man lived in a sort of Garden of Eden, under natural law, even before the establishment of an institution we call government. In this ideal existence men and women had certain rights, called natural rights, because they came naturally to a man or a woman as a human being. When man agreed with his neighbors to form a political society, he gave up certain rights, such as retaliation, in return for protection from the government. However, he retained for himself still other natural rights.

Applying this philosophy to the actual events in the United States, the people formed a government and granted away various powers through the Constitution. Furthermore, the Bill of Rights was enacted to *protect* the rights retained by the people. This amendment was proposed as added insurance or protection for these natural rights.

This amendment simply means that there are other rights, not yet listed, which are still held by the people. The mere listing of some natural rights in the first eight amendments did not exhaust all the natural rights. The federal government cannot interfere with these unlisted rights. Just what these other natural rights are is not easily discovered. They have never been enumerated and in only a few instances do we find that the Supreme Court has expressly stated rights protected by this amendment—the right to engage in political activity, the right to privacy, the right to travel among the states, the right to attend trials. The "right to privacy" concept, made famous in the landmark abortion case of *Roe v. Wade* in 1973 has become a well-used peg upon which to hang constitutional arguments in abortion and related cases during the 1980s and 1990s.

Amendment 10

Proposed September 25, 1789   Ratified December 15, 1791

THE POWERS NOT DELEGATED TO THE UNITED STATES BY THE CONSTITUTION, NOR PROHIBITED BY IT TO THE STATES, ARE RESERVED TO THE STATES RESPECTIVELY, OR TO THE PEOPLE.

This amendment was inserted into the Constitution to make clear and certain that our government was a federal state. Those powers not granted to the national government were reserved to the states or to the people. Just what are these *reserved powers* is hard to say. They would be discovered by a process of elimination, that is, take away all powers given to the national government, plus those powers the states are prohibited from exercising, and what remains would be the reserved powers—such things as marriage, divorce, and education.

These reserved powers, whatever they may be, offer no limitation upon the exercise of the national government's legitimate powers. In a great many areas the national and state governments operate and cooperate in penalizing such activities as interstate transportation of lottery tickets, stolen automobiles, kidnapping, and the trafficking in impure foods and drugs.

Amendment 11

Proposed March 4, 1794   Ratified January 8, 1799

Immunity of States Against Suits

THE JUDICIAL POWER OF THE UNITED STATES SHALL NOT BE CONSTRUED TO EXTEND TO ANY SUIT IN LAW OR EQUITY, COMMENCED OR PROSECUTED AGAINST ONE OF THE UNITED STATES BY CITIZENS OF ANOTHER STATE OR BY CITIZENS OR SUBJECTS OF ANY FOREIGN STATE.

This amendment arose out of a difference of opinion between the states and the Supreme Court. In the original Constitution the jurisdiction of the Supreme Court included "cases and controversies between a State and citizens of another State." At the time of the ratification of the Constitution many persons objected to this clause. They feared that the states would be subjected to numerous suits in federal courts. The constant barrage, even if the states won the suits, would be a great financial burden on their governments. The defenders of the Constitution declared, on the other hand, that this situation would not occur. They said that the states were "sovereign" and could not be sued without their consent. In 1793, however, the Supreme Court did take jurisdiction over a case brought by a citizen of South Carolina against the State of Georgia. The states, and particularly Georgia, were aroused by this action. They thought a number of other suits would be instituted against the debt-ridden states. Thus this amendment was quickly proposed and easily ratified.

Without its expressed consent, a state cannot be sued in the federal courts by either its own citizens, a foreign country, a citizen of another state, or a federally chartered corporation. A state may voluntarily permit itself to be sued, but under such conditions as it sees fit to demand. The only type of suit that may be brought in the federal courts without a state's consent, is one that involves either the United States or another state. The Supreme Court ruled in 1979 that the Constitution does not protect a state from being sued in the courts of another state. Such matters were to be worked out by the states without federal interference. Recent decisions have narrowed a state's immunity by upholding federal legislation that must clearly and explicitly describe the congressional intent and authority.

This amendment does not bar a person from taking a case against a state from its court to the Supreme Court on appeal. For example, if a person is convicted in a state court and he claims his right to counsel (Amendment VI) was violated, he may appeal to the Supreme Court. Also this amendment does not prohibit federal courts from issuing injunctions or other restraining orders against state officials who are acting unconstitutionally. Thus if Citizen A claims his State Treasurer is trying to collect taxes under the authority of an unconstitutional tax law, he *may* be able to get a federal judge to issue an order forbidding the collection of that tax until the validity of the law has been established.

Amendment 12

Proposed December 8, 1803   Ratified September 25, 1804

Election of the President

THE ELECTORS SHALL MEET IN THEIR RESPECTIVE STATES, AND VOTE BY BALLOT FOR PRESIDENT AND VICE-PRESIDENT, ONE OF WHOM, AT LEAST, SHALL NOT BE AN INHABITANT OF THE SAME STATE WITH THEMSELVES; THEY SHALL NAME IN THEIR BALLOTS THE PERSON VOTED FOR AS PRESIDENT, AND IN DISTINCT BALLOTS THE PERSON VOTED FOR AS VICE-PRESIDENT; AND THEY SHALL MAKE DISTINCT LISTS OF ALL PERSONS VOTED FOR AS PRESIDENT, AND OF ALL PERSONS VOTED FOR AS VICE-PRESIDENT, AND OF THE NUMBER OF VOTES FOR EACH, WHICH LISTS THEY SHALL SIGN AND CERTIFY, AND TRANSMIT SEALED TO THE SEAT OF THE GOVERNMENT OF THE UNITED STATES, DIRECTED TO THE PRESIDENT

OF THE SENATE; THE PRESIDENT OF THE SENATE SHALL, IN THE PRESENCE OF THE SENATE AND HOUSE OF REPRESENTATIVES, OPEN ALL THE CERTIFICATES AND THE VOTES SHALL THEN BE COUNTED; THE PERSON HAVING THE GREATEST NUMBER OF VOTES FOR PRESIDENT SHALL BE THE PRESIDENT, IF SUCH NUMBER BE A MAJORITY OF THE WHOLE NUMBER OF ELECTORS APPOINTED; AND IF NO PERSON HAVE SUCH MAJORITY, THEN FROM THE PERSONS HAVING THE HIGHEST NUMBERS NOT EXCEEDING THREE ON THE LIST OF THOSE VOTED FOR AS PRESIDENT, THE HOUSE OF REPRESENTATIVES SHALL CHOOSE IMMEDIATELY, BY BALLOT, THE PRESIDENT. BUT IN CHOOSING THE PRESIDENT, THE VOTES SHALL BE TAKEN BY STATES, THE REPRESENTATION FROM EACH STATE HAVING ONE VOTE; A QUORUM FOR THIS PURPOSE SHALL CONSIST OF A MEMBER OR MEMBERS FROM TWO-THIRDS OF THE STATES, AND A MAJORITY OF ALL THE STATES SHALL BE NECESSARY TO A CHOICE. <u>AND IF THE HOUSE OF REPRESENTATIVES SHALL NOT CHOOSE A PRESIDENT WHENEVER THE RIGHT OF CHOICE SHALL DEVOLVE UPON THEM BEFORE THE FOURTH DAY OF MARCH NEXT FOLLOWING, THEN THE VICE-PRESIDENT SHALL ACT AS PRESIDENT, AS IN THE CASE OF THE DEATH OR OTHER CONSTITUTIONAL DISABILITY OF THE PRESIDENT.</u> THE PERSON HAVING THE GREATEST NUMBER OF VOTES AS VICE-PRESIDENT SHALL BE THE VICE-PRESIDENT, IF SUCH NUMBER BE A MAJORITY OF THE WHOLE NUMBER OF ELECTORS APPOINTED, AND IF NO PERSON HAVE A MAJORITY, THEN FROM THE TWO HIGHEST NUMBERS ON THE LIST, THE SENATE SHALL CHOOSE THE VICE-PRESIDENT; A QUORUM FOR THE PURPOSE SHALL CONSIST OF TWO-THIRDS OF THE WHOLE NUMBER OF SENATORS, AND A MAJORITY OF THE WHOLE NUMBER SHALL BE NECESSARY TO A CHOICE. BUT NO PERSON CONSTITUTIONALLY INELIGIBLE TO THE OFFICE OF PRESIDENT SHALL BE ELIGIBLE TO THAT OF VICE-PRESIDENT OF THE UNITED STATES.

This amendment resulted directly from the unusual election of 1800. The Republican-Democratic candidates received the same number of electoral votes. It was understood by all that Thomas Jefferson was the presidential nominee and Aaron Burr was the vice-presidential candidate. All the Republican-Democratic party electors had placed the names of both men on their ballots, without making any distinction as to office. This was, of course, in accordance with the terms of the original Constitution (Article II, Section 1). Since each candidate received the same number of electoral votes, the election was decided in the House of Representatives. There Alexander Hamilton used his influence on Federalist party members to secure the election of Jefferson on the thirty-sixth ballot. Burr became Vice-President. To prevent such a situation from developing again, the Twelfth Amendment was proposed.

Presidential electors are now required to designate their choices for President and Vice-President. If no candidate receives a majority of the electoral votes, the House of Representatives selects from the highest three candidates (formerly five). The Senate selects the Vice-President, providing no one received a majority, from the top two (formerly three). In the entire history of the United States the House has chosen the President just twice. The first occasion was in 1801 in the unusual Jefferson-Burr situation. The second occasion was in 1825 when our two-party system had become disjointed and five outstanding candidates were in the running for the Presidency. The House finally selected John Quincy Adams. In 1837 the Senate had its first and only opportunity of selecting a Vice-President when it elected Richard M. Johnson.

The underlined portion of this amendment has been replaced by the Twentieth and Twenty-Fifth Amendments.

The Civil War Amendments

Over half a century elapsed before it was necessary to make further changes to the Constitution. The military victory of the North during the Civil War solved the great constitutional question of whether we were a united, indestructible union or merely a league of independent states. However, the pressing problems relating to the social, civil, and political rights of the Negroes were left to the political branches to decide. Congress sought to implant these rights into the Constitution itself and in the short span of five years three amendments were ratified that dealt vitally with social, civil, and political rights of Negroes.

Amendment 13

Proposed January 31, 1865   Ratified December 16, 1865

Slavery

Section 1   Banning Slavery

> NEITHER SLAVERY NOR INVOLUNTARY SERVITUDE, EXCEPT AS A PUNISHMENT FOR CRIME WHEREOF THE PARTY SHALL HAVE BEEN DULY CONVICTED, SHALL EXIST WITHIN THE UNITED STATES, OR ANY PLACE SUBJECT TO THEIR JURISDICTION.

This amendment simply means that neither state governments nor the national government can ever legalize the practice of slavery or involuntary servitude. Furthermore, this amendment acts as a limitation upon individuals and prevents them from subjecting anyone to slavery. Involuntary servitude and slavery mean essentially the same thing—subjection to a master who owns one's person and who may treat a person as property. The meaning of the term is broad enough to cover any peonage or coolie labor system, that is, a compulsory service based on debt. Although Amendment XIII was intended to apply only to Negroes, its language is again so broad as to protect any nationality, race, or color in the continental United States and in our outlying territories and dependencies. The current viability of the Thirteenth Amendment is attested to by the conviction of a Louisiana man in 1979 for "enslaving" two Mexican aliens on his farm.

Note, however, the fact that imprisonment of criminals is not considered involuntary servitude. Nor do certain types of work of a public or semipublic nature come within the meaning of this amendment. For example, seamen are treated as an exceptional class and one who deserts his vessel in violation of a contract may be arrested and either imprisoned or returned to his ship for further service. Also firemen, policemen and members of a train crew have no right to desert their positions during an emergency or in such a way as to endanger life and property under their care.

The governments may exact certain duties from individuals without violating the Thirteenth Amendment. The government can compel military service, adults are required to serve on juries, and in generations past, male citizens had to furnish a stipulated amount of labor annually on the public highways. Of course, a servitude knowingly and willingly entered into cannot be regarded as involuntary servitude.

Section 2   Enforcement

> CONGRESS SHALL HAVE THE POWER TO ENFORCE THIS ARTICLE BY APPROPRIATE LEGISLATION.

This is self-explanatory. Congress, by passing laws that make it a crime for anyone to subject another person to slavery, has provided very stiff punishments for those so convicted. Recent Supreme Court decisions make the Thirteenth Amendment applicable not only to slavery, but also to discrimination of any kind whether practiced by governments or private individuals.

Amendment 14

Proposed June 13, 1866   Ratified July 20, 1868

Political and Civil Rights of Citizens

Section 1   Rights of Citizens

National Citizenship

> ALL PERSONS BORN OR NATURALIZED IN THE UNITED STATES, AND SUBJECT TO THE JURISDICTION THEREOF, ARE CITIZENS OF THE UNITED STATES AND OF THE STATE WHEREIN THEY RESIDE.

The original Constitution used the term "citizen" in several places but never did define who or what a citizen was. This omission became very serious as the slavery issue became more controversial. In 1857 the Supreme Court decided in the famous *Dred Scott* case that blacks were not and never could become citizens of the United States. This clause defines citizenship so as to include blacks, thus reversing the *Dred Scott* decision.

Actually there are three categories of citizens in the United States: (1) those born to citizenship; (2) those upon whom citizenship is bestowed, such as certain Indian and Eskimo tribes; and (3) those who acquire citizenship by naturalization.

The important thing to remember about this clause is the meaning of the phrase "and subject to the jurisdiction thereof." Examples of persons born in the United States but *not* subject to the jurisdiction of the United States would be children born to alien enemies in hostile occupation or to diplomatic representatives of a foreign country. For example, a child born in Washington to the Italian Ambassador would not become a U.S. citizen. However, if a child were born to an English couple vacationing in Florida, the child would be a citizen of the United States. In this case, the English parents are subject to the legal and political control of the U.S. government, though merely visitors. In legal terminology we call this concept of citizenship by reason of place of birth, *jus soli* (law of place).

But what about children born of American parents in foreign countries? Are they citizens? Yes. Our law provides that a child born of an American parent outside the United States is an American citizen. The concept of citizenship by reason of the nationality of the parents is called *jus sanguinis* (law of blood). With two different principles at work—*jus soli* and *jus sanguinis*—it is possible for a person to obtain multiple citizenship. For example, a child born to Japanese parents in the United States obtains both American and Japanese citizenship. Of course, such a person would have to make a choice of citizenship at some time in his life—usually when he reaches twenty-one years of age.

Also notice that most of us in the United States have two

citizenships—national and state. These are two distinct and separate things. A person may be a national citizen and not a citizen of any state (residents of the District of Columbia). The reverse may also be true, though this does not occur as frequently today as fifty or sixty years ago. Finally, citizenship refers to human or natural persons, such as you and me, and not to artificial persons, such as a corporation.

Once obtained, citizenship is hard to lose. Any citizen may voluntarily renounce or give up his or her citizenship. This is called expatriation. Secondly, through federal court procedures the citizenship of a naturalized citizen may be canceled (or denaturalized) if it is proved that fraud or illegal means were used to obtain citizenship. Congressional law provides that certain actions (voting in another country's elections, serving in its armed forces, etc.) would result in the loss of citizenship. This is usually called "presumption of expatriation" and recent Supreme Court decisions have cast considerable doubt on the constitutionality of this law.

Privileges and Immunities of United States Citizens

NO STATE SHALL MAKE OR ENFORCE ANY LAW WHICH SHALL ABRIDGE THE PRIVILEGES OR IMMUNITIES OF CITIZENS OF THE UNITED STATES;

In the previous clause we made the point that national and state citizenship are two distinct things. Now notice that this clause protects only the privileges and immunities of citizens of the *United States*. It makes no mention of privileges and immunities of *state* citizenship.

Shortly after this amendment was adopted the Supreme Court was faced with a very crucial decision that might have changed the nature of our government. The state of Louisiana had granted a corporation a monopoly on the slaughtering of animals for the city of New Orleans. Various butchers protested and took their case all the way to the Supreme Court. They claimed that the business of slaughtering animals was a privilege or immunity of a citizen of the United States and this amendment prohibited states from making laws that denied them their rights. If the Court followed the butchers' line of reasoning, then practically all our civil, political, business, and social rights would come under the protection of Congress. The states, under such reasoning, would be reduced to a shadow of their power. The Supreme Court met the issue head on. It decided that the Congress and the people of the states had not intended to change the nature of our government when they proposed and ratified this amendment. Therefore, the privileges and immunities that are protected by this clause are only those connected with national citizenship (and the slaughtering of animals was not one of them).

Our privileges and immunities as national citizens are not many, nor as important, as are the privileges and immunities coming to us from our state citizenship. As illustrations of our national privileges and immunities, the following are typical: go to the seat of our government, petition Congress, vote for national officers, move freely from state to state, carry on interstate commerce or use the navigable waters of the United States and be protected by the national government while traveling abroad. Thus we see that the bulk of our political and civil rights are derived from state citizenship. Remember that not every right that is listed in the Constitution is a privilege or immunity of U.S. citizenship. Most of these rights apply equally to everyone—aliens and artificial persons, as well as citizens. Also remember that due process of law clauses and the equal protection of the laws clause guarantee us further rights.

Due Process of Law

> NOR SHALL ANY STATE DEPRIVE ANY PERSON OF LIFE,
> LIBERTY, OR PROPERTY, WITHOUT DUE PROCESS OF LAW;

This is the second place in which the *due process of law* clause occurs in the Constitution. It is directed in this instance against the states only. This means that actions taken by state governments, or state officials (and local governments and officials) have to conform to the principles of due process of law.

Our discussion of the due process clause of the Fifth Amendment (protection against the national government) would apply equally well to its meaning in this clause. It has a *procedural* and a *substantive* interpretation. It has never been fully and finally defined.

What is very important is the fact that the Supreme Court has included within the meaning of the due process clause of the Fourteenth Amendment many of the protections of the Bill of Rights. Remember that the Bill of Rights is a restriction on the national government by guaranteeing us certain liberties. Now the Court has extended some of those protections as against encroachment by state governments. All the freedoms of the First Amendment—religion, speech, press, assembly, and petition—are now protected against infringement by both the national and state governments. For example, a state law that required persons soliciting funds for religious purposes to be licensed was held to be unconstitutional. The Court said such a law abridged the liberty of a person without due process of law. The liberty that was abridged was freedom of religion. Thus the First Amendment was included within the meaning of the due process of law clause of the Fourteenth Amendment.

But not every liberty or right listed in the Bill of Rights is protected by the Fourteenth Amendment. The Supreme Court has repeatedly stated that it would decide each case on its own merits in order to see whether due process of law was lacking. Through the years a number of precedents have been established so that we have a pretty good idea which rights are included and which rights are not. Thus the right to counsel, the exclusion of a forced confession, the right to an impartial jury, and the freedom from self-incrimination are a few of the protections afforded by the due process of law clause of the Fourteenth Amendment. On the other hand such things as indictment by grand jury or a trial by twelve people (all guaranteed against infringement by national government) are *not* included within the meaning of the due process of law clause of this amendment.

Equal Protection of the Laws

NOR DENY TO ANY PERSON WITHIN ITS JURISDICTION THE EQUAL PROTECTION OF THE LAWS.

This means that persons shall be entitled to the protection and enjoyment of equal laws. The framers of this amendment intended that this clause would act primarily to protect the rights of African-Americans. However, the term "persons" is used and thus the protection is extended to aliens and corporations (artificial persons) as well as to citizens. In the same manner as the privileges and immunities clause and the due process of law clause, this clause is directed against the states. It does not prohibit private individuals from discriminating against persons. Thus a group of white owners may make a written agreement not to sell their property to African-Americans and nobody could force them to do so. But if one owner did sell to an African-American and the other owner went to the courts to try to hold the seller to his contract, the courts could not enforce the contract. The reason would be that the courts, as agencies of the state government, could not become a party to discrimination.

A new dimension to the protections of this clause has been added in recent years. The Supreme Court has ruled in many cases that no "public" facility may be segregated. By "public" the Court includes not only schools, parks, etc., but also private establishments that are open to or cater to the general public, such as railroads, bus terminals, airlines, etc. In June, 1982, the Supreme Court ruled that the equal protection clause applied to illegal aliens so that their children have a right to free public education.

Equal protection of the laws does not mean that all persons must be treated alike by the state. Some kind of grouping or classification is permitted provided there is a reasonable basis for distinguishing the groups. For example, a state law that requires a person to be twenty-one years of age in order to drink intoxicating beverages is, on its face, discriminatory to those under twenty-one. Yet there are very strong and sound reasons for such a discrimination. The reasonableness of the classification guides the courts. For years the Supreme Court has permitted the segregation of white and African-American students in state colleges and universities, as long as each group had equal facilities. The Court has taken a more realistic look at this situation and has ordered states to admit African-Americans to their universities rather than sending them to all-black schools in other states or to inferior schools within the state. The Court ruled separate or segregated public schools to be discriminatory and therefore unconstitutional. Also, the Court ruled separate or segregated public schools to be discriminatory, therefore unconstitutional, and further, they ruled that the use of busing to achieve racial balance in public schools is an acceptable policy of government. The Court's busing decisions have led to the adoption, in a number of state legislatures, of resolutions requesting a constitutional convention to take such jurisdiction away from the Court. Likewise, the Supreme Court's decisions in the Bakke case (1978) and other cases in upholding the various "quota" or "affirmative action" laws that give a preference to members of minority groups (African-American, Hispanics, Eskimos, Indians, etc.) in admission to universities or employment have generated heated opposition among some conservative organizations.

There is a close connection between this clause and the due process clause. In fact there is a good deal of overlapping. It is difficult to imagine a violation of the equal protection clause that would not at the same time be a violation of the due process clause. There are a number of instances, however, where a violation of the due process clause would not also be a violation of the equal protection clause.

The Supreme Court since the 1960s has invoked the equal protection clause to prohibit unreasonable discrimination based upon sex, ethnic or national origin, race, or minority status. It has also banned unreasonable or arbitrary standards governing the exercise of the voting privilege, has required states to set up almost mathematically equal districts for congressional and state legislative apportionments, and has required that the poor be consulted in managing poverty and welfare programs, and has granted tax relief for low income people. These and other decisions by the Supreme Court have broadened the scope of the Fourteenth Amendment, particularly the Equal Protection of the Law clause, by upholding almost every provision contained in the several Civil Rights Acts passed by Congress since 1957.

Section 2   Apportionment of Representatives

REPRESENTATIVES SHALL BE APPORTIONED AMONG THE
SEVERAL STATES ACCORDING TO THEIR RESPECTIVE NUMBERS,
COUNTING THE WHOLE NUMBER OF PERSONS IN EACH STATE,
EXCLUDING INDIANS NOT TAXED. BUT WHEN THE RIGHT TO VOTE
AT ANY ELECTION FOR THE CHOICE OF ELECTORS FOR PRESIDENT
AND VICE-PRESIDENT OF THE UNITED STATES, REPRESENTATIVES
IN CONGRESS, THE EXECUTIVE AND JUDICIAL OFFICERS OF A STATE,
OR THE MEMBERS OF THE LEGISLATURE THEREOF, IS DENIED TO
ANY OF THE MALE INHABITANTS OF SUCH STATE, BEING TWENTY-
ONE YEARS OF AGE, AND CITIZENS OF THE UNITED STATES, OR IN
ANY WAY ABRIDGED, EXCEPT FOR PARTICIPATION IN REBELLION,
OR OTHER CRIME, THE BASIS OF REPRESENTATION THEREIN SHALL
BE REDUCED IN THE PROPORTION WHICH THE NUMBER OF SUCH
MALE CITIZENS SHALL BEAR TO THE WHOLE NUMBER OF MALE
CITIZENS TWENTY-ONE YEARS OF AGE IN SUCH STATE.

The first sentence of this section repeals a portion of Section 2 of Article I which counted African-Americans as three-fifths of a person for purposes of representation and taxation. Furthermore, since 1935 Indians have been subject to the federal income tax, so that all persons are now counted for apportionment purposes.

The remainder of this section was intended to be the weapon that would force southern states to extend the voting privilege to African-Americans. If these states continued to discriminate, the framers of this amendment reasoned, they would lose representation in the House. Thus not only would the South lose power in Congress, but it would also lose influence in presidential elections. But this threat never worked. The South continued to disfranchise African-Americans and the Fifteenth Amendment had to be adopted.

The reduction of representation threatened by this section has never materialized. Whenever it came up in the Congress, the southern states would point to literacy tests in northern states and charge discrimination. There has never been a serious effort by northerners in Congress to push this penalty. Even the courts had sidestepped the issue by declaring that apportionment is a political question that Congress must determine. Thus this section appears to be a "dead letter" insofar as enforcement is concerned.

Section 3   Disqualifying Confederate Officials

NO PERSON SHALL BE A SENATOR OR REPRESENTATIVE IN CONGRESS, OR ELECTOR OF PRESIDENT AND VICE-PRESIDENT, OR HOLD ANY OFFICE, CIVIL OR MILITARY, UNDER THE UNITED STATES, OR UNDER ANY STATE, WHO, HAVING PREVIOUSLY TAKEN AN OATH, AS A MEMBER OF CONGRESS, OR AS AN OFFICER OF THE UNITED STATES, OR AS A MEMBER OF ANY STATE LEGISLATURE, OR AS AN EXECUTIVE OR JUDICIAL OFFICER OF ANY STATE, TO SUPPORT THE CONSTITUTION OF THE UNITED STATES, SHALL HAVE ENGAGED IN INSURRECTION OR REBELLION AGAINST THE SAME, OR GIVEN AID OR COMFORT TO THE ENEMIES THEREOF. BUT CONGRESS MAY BY A VOTE OF TWO-THIRDS OF EACH HOUSE REMOVE SUCH DISABILITY.

The "Radical Congress" sought to punish the leaders of the Confederacy with this section. Later Congress passed laws (in 1869 and 1872) that exempted various individuals from the effect of this section. Finally, on June 6, 1898, Congress completely removed the political disability.

Section 4   Validity of the Public Debt

THE VALIDITY OF THE PUBLIC DEBT OF THE UNITED STATES, AUTHORIZED BY LAW, INCLUDING DEBTS INCURRED FOR PAYMENT OF PENSIONS AND BOUNTIES FOR SERVICES IN SUPPRESSING INSURRECTION OR REBELLION, SHALL NOT BE QUESTIONED. BUT NEITHER THE UNITED STATES NOR ANY STATE SHALL ASSUME OR PAY ANY DEBT OR OBLIGATION INCURRED IN AID OF INSURRECTION OR REBELLION AGAINST THE UNITED STATES, OR ANY CLAIM FOR THE LOSS OR EMANCIPATION OF ANY SLAVE; BUT ALL SUCH DEBTS, OBLIGATIONS AND CLAIMS SHALL BE HELD ILLEGAL AND VOID.

This section reaffirms the willingness of the U.S. government to pay the debts incurred by it while fighting the War. Furthermore, it makes clear that the U.S. government would not be responsible for debts contracted by the Confederacy or by any of the southern states. In fact, this section actually prevents the southern states from paying their war debts, even if they wanted to.

Section 5   Enforcement

THE CONGRESS SHALL HAVE POWER TO ENFORCE, BY APPROPRIATE LEGISLATION, THE PROVISIONS OF THIS ARTICLE.

The power possessed by the Congress by reason of this clause gives it authority to prevent *states* from denying due process of law or equal protection of the laws. This section does not give Congress the power to legislate on everything or anything. For example, in 1875 Congress passed a law (under authority of this section) forbidding proprietors of hotels, theaters, or other places of public resort from discriminating against or refusing to accommodate persons because of their race or color. The Supreme Court declared the law unconstitutional because Congress has no power to legislate with respect to discrimination by *individuals.* However, when a Virginia judge systematically excluded African-Americans from his juries, the Supreme Court said that this action may be punished by Congress because it denied equal protection of the laws. In the 1875 case Congress tried to regulate *individual* conduct, but in the Virginia case the judge was an officer of the *state* and came under this section. Congress passed the Civil Rights Act of 1964, which forbids discrimination in public accommodations. Under powers given to Congress by other sections of the Constitution, individual as well as state interference with the rights of U.S. citizens may be prevented. Yet, recent decisions, especially the Bakke case (1978), may indicate a trend toward the constitutional acceptability of Congress's use of this enforcement section to ban discrimination or achieve equal protection of the laws.

Amendment 15

Proposed February 26, 1869   Ratified March 30, 1870

Right to Vote

Section 1   Negro Suffrage

THE RIGHT OF CITIZENS OF THE UNITED STATES TO VOTE SHALL NOT BE DENIED OR ABRIDGED BY THE UNITED STATES OR BY ANY STATE ON ACCOUNT OF RACE, COLOR, OR PREVIOUS CONDITION OF SERVITUDE.

This amendment was added to our Constitution in order to protect the political rights of Negroes. Notice that the wording of this amendment is negative. It does not say that all African-Americans are entitled to vote. It says that *states* shall not use race, color, or slavery as bases for disqualifying a person from voting.

The adoption of this amendment did not result in the immediate enfranchisement of large numbers of African-Americans. In fact, the history of most southern states since 1870 has been notable for the many attempts on their part to evade the clear meaning of the amendment. The most notorious evasive devices have been declared unconstitutional by the Supreme Court—particularly the "grandfather clause" (exemption of illiterate whites from a literacy test if they could show that they or their ancestors had been voters prior to January 1, 1867) and the "white primary" (restriction of membership in the Democratic Party to whites only). The more refined techniques of long residence requirements, tricky poll tax payments, literacy, and understanding tests are harder to prove as discriminatory to the African-American alone. In spite of these obstacles, the various Civil Rights Acts, favorable court decisions, and significant changes in attitude and behavior have resulted in great strides in black political participation. In the eleven southern states, for example, black voter registration increased from approximately 1,400,000 or 29 percent of the voting age population in 1960 to over 4,100,000 or 63 percent by 1976. Likewise, black elected public officials grew from a total of only 1,472 throughout the United States in 1970 to over 7,400 in 1991, including two governors, 314 mayors and over 2,000 black women elected officials, and to 8,015 in 1993.

Section 2   Enforcement

THE CONGRESS SHALL HAVE POWER TO ENFORCE THIS ARTICLE BY APPROPRIATE LEGISLATION.

In the past the Supreme Court was very reluctant to uphold legislation passed under the authority of this section. Given the authority of this section, however, Congress passed the Voting Rights Act of 1965, and the courts have upheld almost every provision of the basic law as well as the several amendments, passed in 1970, 1975, and 1982. Thus, state literacy tests were regulated, registration procedures supervised, residence requirements liberalized, and the entire voting process was subjected to review so that unreasonable discrimination would be eliminated, black vote would not be diluted, uniform standards were set for federal jurors, discrimination was prohibited in the advertising, sale, or rental of housing, and various types of discriminatory employment practices by business groups were forbidden.

Amendment 16

Proposed July 12, 1909   Ratified February 25, 1913

Income Tax

THE CONGRESS SHALL HAVE POWER TO LAY AND COLLECT TAXES ON INCOMES, FROM WHATEVER SOURCE DERIVED, WITHOUT APPORTIONMENT AMONG THE SEVERAL STATES, AND WITHOUT REGARD TO ANY CENSUS OR ENUMERATION.

This is another amendment that has had the effect of nullifying a Supreme Court decision. A tax on incomes had been enacted during the Civil War. It was not until 1881, many years after the tax had expired, that the validity of Congress's action was challenged. The Supreme Court held, however, that a tax on incomes was an *indirect tax* and completely within the powers given to Congress by the Constitution. In 1894 Congress enacted another income tax law. This time it was immediately challenged. The Supreme Court, in a 5–4 decision, ruled that a tax on incomes derived from property was a *direct tax*. Such a tax, the Constitution requires to be apportioned among the states according to population (Article I, Sections 2 and 9). Also the Court said income from state or municipal bonds could not be taxed. Excluding these sources from an income tax would make such a law impractical and unfair; therefore agitation continued for an Amendment that would clearly give Congress the power to tax any income. After much intensive argument in Congress and in the states, the Sixteenth Amendment became law in 1913.

Actually this amendment did not give Congress a new source of taxation. It took a source of revenue out of one category (direct tax) and placed it in another (indirect tax). The phrase "from whatever source derived" has been held to give Congress the power to tax as income monies gained by illegal or illicit means (gambling, extortion, etc.). Congress also has the power to allow such deductions and exemptions as it feels are proper.

Amendment 17

Proposed May 13, 1912   Ratified May 31, 1913

Popular Election of Senators
This amendment brought to a successful conclusion a long period of argument and agitation. As the suffrage was extended, public opinion began to demand that Senators be more responsive to the public will. This could best be accomplished by making them subject to popular election the same as Representatives. Under the original method of selection (by state legislatures), a number of abuses had become standard practice. There were often deadlocks between the

two houses over specific candidates. Corrupt political parties and corrupt interest groups were able to influence the legislators.

In many states these abuses had been corrected even before the Amendment was proposed. Some states had amended their direct primary laws to permit the people to vote on senatorial candidates. Then the legislature, guided by this popular vote, could choose between the primary winners. A few states went so far as to bind the legislature to select candidate having the highest number of votes. So far had these practices developed at the state level that by the time the amendment was introduced twenty-nine states provided some means of popular control over Senators. It is easily seen why it took only a year for approval to be given by the states.

Section 1.   Popular Election

THE SENATE OF THE UNITED STATES SHALL BE COMPOSED OF TWO SENATORS FROM EACH STATE, ELECTED BY THE PEOPLE THEREOF FOR SIX YEARS; AND EACH SENATOR SHALL HAVE ONE VOTE. THE ELECTORS IN EACH STATE SHALL HAVE THE QUALIFICATIONS REQUIRED FOR ELECTORS OF THE MOST NUMEROUS BRANCH OF THE STATE LEGISLATURE.

The first part of this clause merely reenacts a portion of the original Constitution. The remainder of the clause means that those persons eligible to vote for members of the state legislature also have the necessary qualifications to vote in senatorial elections.

Section 2.   Filling Vacancies

WHEN VACANCIES HAPPEN IN THE REPRESENTATION OF ANY STATE IN THE SENATE, THE EXECUTIVE AUTHORITY OF SUCH STATE SHALL ISSUE WRITS OF ELECTION TO FILL SUCH VACANCIES: PROVIDED, THAT THE LEGISLATURE OF ANY STATE MAY EMPOWER THE EXECUTIVE THEREOF TO MAKE TEMPORARY APPOINTMENTS UNTIL THE PEOPLE FILL THE VACANCY BY ELECTION AS THE LEGISLATURE MAY DIRECT.

This section also reenacts previous sections of the original Constitution. A slight change occurs because of the new method of elections. (see Article I, Section 3) .

Section 3.   Effective Date

THIS AMENDMENT SHALL NOT BE SO CONSTRUED AS TO AFFECT THE ELECTION OR TERM OF ANY SENATOR CHOSEN BEFORE IT BECOMES VALID AS PART OF THE CONSTITUTION.

This was a necessary provision; otherwise, a number of duly elected Senators might have lost their legal office.

Amendment 18

Proposed December 18, 1917   Ratified January 29, 1919

Prohibition of Intoxicating Liquors

There always have been a number of people in the United States who believed that intoxicating liquors are harmful and sinful. The influence of these people varied from section to section in the country and even within a single state. Since 1872 a group called the Prohibition Party has nominated a candidate for the presidency. The prohibitionists always have been active in politics and have achieved notable success in a few states. Nationally they had little success until the advent of World War I. Under the leadership of the Anti-Saloon League, one of the most powerful pressure groups in our history, the prohibitionists secured the enactment of a number of restrictive laws in Congress. Alcohol was an essential war material, grain also was vital to our war effort, and a moral case against drinking by servicemen could be effective. Thus the Prohibition Amendment slipped into our Constitution.

But the passage of the amendment did not solve the drinking problem. If anything, the amendment created more problems. Large numbers of persons were deadly opposed to the amendment. While seeking its repeal, they often evaded its provisions. The making and distributing of illegal liquor, bootlegging as it was called, almost became respectable. Numerous cases were reported of deaths and injuries resulting from impure bootleg liquor. Criminals and gangsters flourished under the general evasion of the laws. Prohibition was almost impossible to enforce. The states and the federal government had to appropriate large amounts of money to hire investigators; yet this was largely wasted because the people would not stand for such a regulation of their personal habits. Finally, this amendment was repealed by the Twenty-First Amendment in 1933.

Section 1   Prohibiting Intoxicating Liquors

AFTER ONE YEAR FROM THE RATIFICATION OF THIS ARTICLE THE MANUFACTURE, SALE, OR TRANSPORTATION OF INTOXICATING LIQUORS WITHIN, THE IMPORTATION THEREOF INTO, OR THE EXPORTATION THEREOF FROM THE UNITED STATES AND ALL TERRITORY SUBJECT TO THE JURISDICTION THEREOF FOR BEVERAGE PURPOSES IS HEREBY PROHIBITED.

Note that this bans the manufacture and sale for beverage purposes. Alcohol and similar products could be manufactured for commercial and industrial purposes. The problem was to make sure it was used for just these purposes.

Section 2   Enforcement

THE CONGRESS AND THE SEVERAL STATES SHALL HAVE CONCURRENT POWER TO ENFORCE THIS ARTICLE BY APPROPRIATE LEGISLATION.

Congress passed the National Prohibition Act. Each state had its own law. A person caught bootlegging could be subject to trial and punishment by both the national and state governments. This would not involve double jeopardy because the one crime violated the laws of two governments.

Section 3 Time Limit

THIS ARTICLE SHALL BE INOPERATIVE UNLESS IT SHALL HAVE BEEN RATIFIED AS AN AMENDMENT TO THE CONSTITUTION BY THE LEGISLATURES OF THE SEVERAL STATES, AS PROVIDED IN THE CONSTITUTION, WITHIN SEVEN YEARS FROM THE DATE OF THE SUBMISSION HEREOF TO THE STATES BY THE CONGRESS.

The amendment was ratified well within the seven-year time limit.

Amendment 19

Proposed June 4, 1919   Ratified August 26, 1920

Women's Suffrage

Women had been fighting for the right to vote as early as the Jacksonian era. The question came up again during the agitation over slavery. No real success was obtained until 1869 when the Territory of Wyoming extended the privilege of voting to women. Upon its admission as a state in 1890, Wyoming retained women's suffrage. Three other western states had joined Wyoming by the turn of the century. After a few unsucessful attempts, five other western states had extended voting rights to women by the eve of World War I. In addition, a few other states had permitted women to vote in local elections.

This state-by-state approach was a hard and drawn-out struggle. A change in tactics was in order and the women concentrated on a constitutional amendment. This would enfranchise all the women in every state. Tremendous pressure was brought to bear on Congress and the President and finally the Nineteenth Amendment was proposed.

Section 1 Women's Suffrage

THE RIGHT OF CITIZENS OF THE UNITED STATES TO VOTE SHALL NOT BE DENIED OR ABRIDGED BY THE UNITED STATES OR BY ANY STATE ON ACCOUNT OF SEX.

Section 2   Enforcement

CONGRESS SHALL HAVE POWER TO ENFORCE THIS ARTICLE
BY APPROPRIATE LEGISLATION.

This amendment operates in the same manner as the Fifteenth. It does not positively give all women the privilege of voting. It acts negatively on the states. No state may use sex as a basis for disqualifying persons otherwise entitled to vote. The prohibition applies equally to the national government, though this has relatively little significance, since suffrage qualifications are primarily the responsibility of the states.

There has been no need for Congress to pass legislation on this matter.

Amendment 20

Proposed March 3, 1932   Ratified February 6, 1933

Terms of Office—Lame Duck Amendment

For decades congressmen, party leaders, writers, and other interested citizens were concerned with the long period of time between the November election and the March inauguration of the President. These four months presented serious problems of leadership, especially if the presidency was to change hands and parties. The outgoing president would be reluctant to act and the incoming one would not have the power to act. In times of crisis this situation could prove disastrous to the country.

Furthermore, under the original Constitution, a short session of Congress was required from December to March. In a number of elections, congressmen who had been defeated at the polls in November continued to serve during this short session. In time these defeated congressmen became known as "lame ducks" and the short session was commonly called "the lame duck session." Meanwhile, newly elected, congressmen could not begin their service to their constituents until the following December, thirteen months after their election! There might have been a need for a short session and late inaugural during the early period of our history because of poor transportation facilities, but twentieth century transportation and communication systems could no longer justify such delay. Accordingly, the Congress, under the leadership of Senator George Norris, proposed the Twentieth Amendment.

Section 1   Terms of Office

THE TERMS OF THE PRESIDENT AND VICE-PRESIDENT SHALL END AT NOON ON THE 20TH DAY OF JANUARY, AND THE TERMS OF SENATORS AND REPRESENTATIVES AT NOON ON THE 3RD DAY OF JANUARY, OF THE YEAR IN WHICH SUCH TERMS OF THEIR SUCCESSORS SHALL THEN BEGIN.

This section changes the dates for the beginning of the presidential and congressional terms of office. Thus the Congress (1934-36) and President Franklin D. Roosevelt had shorter terms than any of their predecessors.

Section 2   Convening of Congress

THE CONGRESS SHALL ASSEMBLE AT LEAST ONCE IN EVERY YEAR, AND SUCH MEETING SHALL BEGIN AT NOON ON THE 3RD DAY OF JANUARY, UNLESS THEY SHALL BY LAW APPOINT A DIFFERENT DAY.

This session eliminates the short or lame duck session. It also does away with the need for many special sessions. Congress may still meet in more than one session each year if the President calls them.

Section 3   Succession to the Presidency

IF, AT THE TIME FIXED FOR THE BEGINNING OF THE TERM OF THE PRESIDENT, THE PRESIDENT ELECT SHALL HAVE DIED, THE VICE-PRESIDENT ELECT SHALL BECOME PRESIDENT. IF A PRESIDENT SHALL NOT HAVE BEEN CHOSEN BEFORE THE TIME FIXED FOR THE

BEGINNING OF HIS TERM, OR IF THE PRESIDENT ELECT SHALL HAVE
FAILED TO QUALIFY, THEN THE VICE-PRESIDENT ELECT SHALL ACT
AS PRESIDENT UNTIL A PRESIDENT SHALL HAVE QUALIFIED; AND
THE CONGRESS MAY BY LAW PROVIDE FOR THE CASE WHEREIN
NEITHER A PRESIDENT ELECT NOR A VICE-PRESIDENT ELECT SHALL
HAVE QUALIFIED, DECLARING WHO SHALL THEN ACT AS PRESIDENT,
OR THE MANNER IN WHICH ONE WHO IS TO ACT SHALL BE SELECTED,
AND SUCH PERSON SHALL ACT ACCORDINGLY UNTIL A PRESIDENT
OR VICE-PRESIDENT SHALL HAVE QUALIFIED.

Notice that this section provides for persons to serve as President
and to act as President. There is a difference between being the
President and acting as President until such time as someone shall
properly fill the office.

If the President-elect dies between the time Congress counts the
electoral vote (January 6) and the inauguration (January 20), then the
Vice-President-elect becomes the President. If, however, the House
of Representatives has not reached a decision on a presidential election
by January 20 or the successful presidential candidate lacks the
constitutional qualifications (Article 2, Section 1), then the Vice-
President-elect acts as President until a President qualifies for the
office.

This section also empowers Congress to provide for the situation
when neither the President-elect nor Vice-President-elect qualifies.
It was not until 1948, upon the urging of President Harry S Truman,
that Congress acted to fulfill this duty. The Presidential Succession
Act of 1948 extended the line of succession to first the Speaker of
the House, the President pro tempore of the Senate, and then the
heads of executive departments in the order of the creation of each
department. Like those who serve as President and Vice-President
whoever acts as President must meet the constitutional qualifications
of the office.

Section 4   Providing for Vacancies

THE CONGRESS MAY BY LAW PROVIDE FOR THE CASE OF THE
DEATH OF ANY OF THE PERSONS FROM WHOM THE HOUSE OF

REPRESENTATIVES MAY CHOOSE A PRESIDENT WHENEVER THE
RIGHT OF CHOICE SHALL HAVE DEVOLVED UPON THEM, AND FOR
THE CASE OF THE DEATH OF ANY OF THE PERSONS FROM WHOM
THE SENATE MAY CHOOSE A VICE-PRESIDENT WHEN EVER THE
RIGHT OF CHOICE SHALL HAVE DEVOLVED UPON THEM.

Congress has not acted as of this date upon this section. The situation would occur if no candidate received a majority of the electoral votes. The House then selects a President from the top three candidates. What would happen if one of these three should die before the House reached a decision? This section gives Congress the power to provide for such an emergency. The Twenty-Fifth Amendment has a bearing on this section, but a constitutional gap still exists in filling vacancies between the election in November and the counting of the electoral vote in January.

Section 5 Effective Date

SECTIONS 1 AND 2 SHALL TAKE EFFECT ON THE 15TH DAY
OF OCTOBER FOLLOWING THE RATIFICATION OF THIS ARTICLE.

Section 6 Time Limit

THIS ARTICLE SHALL BE INOPERATIVE UNLESS IT SHALL HAVE
BEEN RATIFIED AS AN AMENDMENT TO THE CONSTITUTION BY THE
LEGISLATURES OF THREE-FOURTHS OF THE SEVERAL STATES WITHIN
SEVEN YEARS FROM THE DATE OF ITS SUBMISSION.

Amendment 21

Proposed February 20, 1933   Ratified December 5, 1933

Repeal of Prohibition

The enforcement of the Eighteenth Amendment proved to be more difficult and expensive than Congress or the people had anticipated. Legal manufacture and sale of intoxicating liquors were easily regulated, but in their place there developed thousands of illegal sources. Bootleggers and criminals moved into the industry and brought with them their practices of bloodshed and violence. Police of the cities and states were no match for the nationwide crime and liquor gangs. The federal police officials were hard-pressed to keep up with their activities.

There always had been large and vocal groups, primarily in urban areas, opposed to prohibition. They intensified their efforts to get the amendment repealed. Governor Alfred Smith, the Democratic presidential candidate in 1928, though running on a "dry" platform, made his "wet" position clear. Finally in the 1932 campaign both parties came out in favor of repeal.

Section 1   Repeal of Prohibition

THE EIGHTEENTH ARTICLE OF AMENDMENT TO THE CONSTITUTION OF THE UNITED STATES IS HEREBY REPEALED.

This section nullifies any and all powers that had been granted to either Congress or the states by the Eighteenth Amendment. This meant that prosecutions for violations of the National Prohibition Act (including proceedings on appeal, pending an appeal, or begun after the date of repeal) had to be dismissed because the courts no longer had jurisdiction on that subject.

Section 2   State Prohibition Laws

THE TRANSPORTATION OR IMPORTATION INTO ANY STATE, TERRITORY, OR POSSESSION OF THE UNITED STATES FOR DELIVERY OR USE THEREIN OF INTOXICATING LIQUORS, IN VIOLATION OF THE LAWS THEREOF, IS HEREBY PROHIBITED.

This section gives a state the right and the power to prevent liquor from being imported into or used within the state. That is, if the people of a state want to ban intoxicating liquors, they may do so, without fear of violating Congress's power over interstate commerce.

Section 3   Time Limit

THIS ARTICLE SHALL BE INOPERATIVE UNLESS IT SHALL HAVE BEEN RATIFIED AS AN AMENDMENT TO THE CONSTITUTION BY CONVENTIONS IN THE SEVERAL STATES, AS PROVIDED IN THE CONSTITUTION, WITHIN SEVEN YEARS FROM THE DATE OF THE SUBMISSION HEREOF TO THE STATES BY CONGRESS.

Amendment 22

Proposed March 24, 1947   Ratified March 1, 1951

Presidential Tenure

Under the terms of the original Constitution a person could become President as many times as the people would elect him. From the very start of our constitutional history a custom was established whereby a person served only two terms. George Washington started the tradition and when Jefferson, Madison, and Monroe followed, the "two-term tradition" took on the characteristics of fundamental law. The tradition did not go unchallenged. In 1884 Ulysses S. Grant sought a nomination for a third term but failed to receive it. In 1912 Theodore Roosevelt sought the office for a third time and was just barely defeated. Finally in 1940 Franklin D. Roosevelt ran and was elected for a third term; and also a fourth term in 1944. A number of persons looked upon Roosevelt's action as a violation of the spirit of the Constitution, although there was no question of the legality of his running for office a third time. Within a short time after Roosevelt's death, the Twenty-Second Amendment was proposed and adopted.

Section 1   Limit of Two Terms

NO PERSON SHALL BE ELECTED TO THE OFFICE OF THE PRESIDENT MORE THAN TWICE, AND NO PERSON WHO HAS HELD THE OFFICE OF PRESIDENT, OR ACTED AS PRESIDENT, FOR MORE THAN TWO YEARS OF A TERM TO WHICH SOME OTHER PERSON WAS ELECTED PRESIDENT SHALL BE ELECTED TO THE OFFICE OF

THE PRESIDENT MORE THAN ONCE. BUT THIS ARTICLE SHALL NOT APPLY TO ANY PERSON HOLDING THE OFFICE OF PRESIDENT WHEN THIS ARTICLE WAS PROPOSED BY THE CONGRESS, AND SHALL NOT PREVENT ANY PERSON WHO MAY BE HOLDING THE OFFICE OF PRESIDENT, OR ACTING AS PRESIDENT, DURING THE TERM WITHIN WHICH THIS ARTICLE BECOMES OPERATIVE FROM HOLDING THE OFFICE OF PRESIDENT OR ACTING AS PRESIDENT DURING THE REMAINDER OF SUCH TERM.

This amendment sets a limit on the number of terms, and the number of years, a person may serve as President. If a person is originally elected to the office, he may serve no more than two full terms, that is, a maximum of eight years.

If, upon the death of the incumbent President, or for some other reason, a person succeeds to the office with *two or more* years remaining to fulfill, then he may serve only one additional full term. In such an instance, a person would serve a maximum of six years. However, if a person succeeds to the office with *less* than two years to the end of the term, then he would be eligible to serve two full terms. In a case of this type, a person would be permitted to serve a maximum of ten years less one day.

When this amendment was proposed and ratified, Harry S Truman was President. Even though he had served more than three years of Franklin D. Roosevelt's 1944 term and was completing a full four-year term of his own, the amendment was worded so as not to apply to him. Since Truman chose not to run in 1952, and since Dwight D. Eisenhower was elected, the amendment applied to Eisenhower and all future presidents.

Section 2   Time Limit

THIS ARTICLE SHALL BE INOPERATIVE UNLESS IT SHALL HAVE BEEN RATIFIED AS AN AMENDMENT TO THE CONSTITUTION BY THE LEGISLATURES OF THREE-FOURTHS OF THE SEVERAL STATES WITHIN SEVEN YEARS FROM THE DATE OF ITS SUBMISSION TO THE STATES BY THE CONGRESS.

Amendment 23

Proposed June 21, 1960   Ratified March 29, 1961

Electoral Vote for the District of Columbia

Years of agitation and frustration for the residents of the District of Columbia climaxed in 1961 with the ratification of the Twenty-Third Amendment. Although the permanent residents of the District were citizens of the United States, subject to all the laws, nevertheless they were denied the privilege of voting for federal officials. The Twenty-Third Amendment changed all this.

Permanent residents now may vote for presidential and vice-presidential candidates. To be sure, temporary or transient residents of the District could vote in their home states, but the tens of thousands of native Washingtonians could not. The Twenty-Third Amendment, however, did not give the residents of the District any home rule or power to run their own local government. This was accomplished in 1975 when a congressional authorized home rule charter became effective.

Section 1   Apportioning Electoral Votes

THE DISTRICT CONSTITUTING THE SEAT OF GOVERNMENT OF THE UNITED STATES SHALL APPOINT IN SUCH MANNER AS THE CONGRESS MAY DIRECT:

A NUMBER OF ELECTORS OF PRESIDENT AND VICE-PRESIDENT EQUAL TO THE WHOLE NUMBER OF SENATORS AND REPRESENTATIVES IN CONGRESS TO WHICH THE DISTRICT WOULD BE ENTITLED IF IT WERE A STATE, BUT IN NO EVENT MORE THAN THE LEAST POPULOUS STATE; THEY SHALL BE IN ADDITION TO THOSE APPOINTED BY THE STATES, BUT THEY SHALL BE CONSIDERED, FOR THE PURPOSE OF THE ELECTION OF PRESIDENT AND VICE PRESIDENT, TO BE ELECTORS APPOINTED BY A STATE; AND THEY SHALL MEET IN THE DISTRICT AND PERFORM SUCH DUTIES AS PROVIDED BY THE TWELFTH ARTICLE OF AMENDMENT.

Note that this section sets no specific number of electoral votes for the District. Rather it ties the District's vote to that of the least populous state. Since the minimum number of electoral votes accorded a state is three (one for each Senator and one for the Representative) and the least populous state, Wyoming, is entitled to no more than the minimum, then the voters of the District of Columbia can choose three electors in each presidential election.

In 1978 Congress sent to the states a proposed constitutional amendment (Twenty-Eighth) which, in effect, would treat the District "as though it were a state." The District would be allocated two Senators and as many Representatives as its population would entitle it to under the existing apportionment formula. These officials would be the equals, in all respects, to other Senators and Representatives and would, of course, provide the basis for the number of electors the District would have in the presidential electoral college. Less than a dozen states had ratified this amendment by the time limit set, 1985, which probably means that this proposal is constitutionally dead.

Section 2   Implementation

THE CONGRESS SHALL HAVE POWER TO ENFORCE THIS ARTICLE BY APPROPRIATE LEGISLATION.

Acting under the authority of this section Congress passed enabling legislation establishing voting qualification, election calendars, and nominating procedures. An interesting feature of this law deals with the regulation of party finances.

Amendment 24

Proposed August 27, 1962   Ratified January 23, 1964

Barring Poll Tax in Federal Elections

Numerous efforts had been made to ban the poll tax. Several statutes were proposed in Congress and on five occasions a bill actually passed the House of Representatives only to be defeated in the Senate. In 1962 a proposed constitutional amendment received the necessary two-thirds majority in both houses and was submitted to the states for their approval.

Most states had abandoned the poll tax as a qualification for voting long before the Twenty-Fourth Amendment was passed. In fact only five states (Alabama, Arkansas, Mississippi, Texas, and Virginia) had a poll tax tied to the voting privilege at the time the Amendment was ratified.

Section 1   Barring Poll Tax in Federal Elections

THE RIGHT OF CITIZENS OF THE UNITED STATES TO VOTE IN ANY PRIMARY OR OTHER ELECTION FOR PRESIDENT OR VICE-PRESIDENT, FOR ELECTORS FOR PRESIDENT OR VICE PRESIDENT, OR FOR SENATOR OR REPRESENTATIVE IN CONGRESS, SHALL NOT BE DENIED OR BRIDGED BY THE UNITED STATES OR ANY STATE BY REASONS OF FAILURE TO PAY ANY POLL TAX OR OTHER TAX.

There are several points to note in this section. First, the protections of this amendment apply only to federal elections— elections where federal officers are involved. However, in 1966 the Supreme Court, through the equal-protection-of-the-laws clause, banned states from using a poll tax in state and local elections. Secondly, primary elections are also included within the ban. Finally, the amendment bans the use of a poll tax (which is a head tax or per capita tax) as a prerequisite to participating in the electoral process. The amendment does not outlaw poll taxes per se. Several states levy a poll tax but a person would not lose his or her voting privilege by failing to pay this tax. The Twenty-Fourth Amendment says that a state cannot tie the payment of a tax to the voting franchise.

Section 2   Implementation

THE CONGRESS SHALL HAVE THE POWER TO ENFORCE THIS ARTICLE BY APPROPRIATE LEGISLATION.

Amendment 25

Proposed July 6, 1965   Ratified February 10, 1967

Appointment of Vice-President—Presidential Disability

Serious gaps existed in our constitutional system with respect to presidential succession, failure of candidates to qualify for the presidency or vice presidency, vacancies in office, and the question of what to do in the event the President became so sick or injured that he could not perform the duties of the office.

The Twentieth Amendment and congressional legislation helped to stabilize the question of succession. The Twenty-Fifth Amendment was passed to give constitutional protection to an established practice and to provide guidelines in the unfortunate instance where a President becomes disabled.

Section 1   Vice-President Becomes President

IN CASE OF THE REMOVAL OF THE PRESIDENT FROM OFFICE OR OF HIS DEATH OR RESIGNATION, THE VICE-PRESIDENT SHALL BECOME PRESIDENT.

John Tyler was the first Vice-President to be faced with the situation of the President dying in office. The immediate question was whether Tyler became the President with all rights, powers, authority, etc., or whether he was merely the acting President until such time as someone qualified as President. Tyler took the position that he became President, thus setting a precedent. His position was accepted by the Congress, courts, and citizens. The seven other vice-presidents (Millard Fillmore, 1850; Andrew Johnson, 1865; Chester A. Arthur, 1881; Theodore Roosevelt, 1901; Calvin Coolidge, 1923; Harry S Truman, 1945; Lyndon B. Johnson, 1963) who succeeded to the office upon the death of the President followed Tyler's precedent. Thus this section merely confirms and gives constitutional sanction to an established practice.

After Richard M. Nixon resigned on August 9, 1974, the Chief

Justice of the Supreme Court immediately swore in Gerald R. Ford as the 38th President of the United States.

Section 2   Nomination and Confirmation of Vice-President

WHENEVER THERE IS A VACANCY IN THE OFFICE OF THE VICE-PRESIDENT, THE PRESIDENT SHALL NOMINATE A VICE-PRESIDENT WHO SHALL TAKE OFFICE UPON CONFIRMATION BY A MAJORITY VOTE OF BOTH HOUSES OF CONGRESS.

Seven vice-presidents have died in office and two (John C. Calhoun, 1832, Spiro T. Agnew, 1973) have resigned. If the nine vice-presidents who succeeded to the presidency are added to these nine, it results in a total of eighteen vacancies in the office of Vice-President in our history. In many of these instances, two or three years elapsed before the office was filled by the regular elective process. Although the Twentieth Amendment provided for the succession of the presidency through the Vice-President, Speaker of the House, President pro tempore of the Senate, and on through the various cabinet positions, no such succession procedure covered vice-presidential vacancies.

The procedure set up by this section is relatively simple. The President nominates a person and submits his choice to the Congress, which votes on the nominee. A majority vote, a quorum being present, is all that is required in each house to confirm the appointment. In form, the procedure parallels the political practice where a presidential candidate chooses his vice-presidential running-mate and the nominating convention invariably approves his choice. In filling the vice-presidential vacancy under this section, the Congress would be comparable to the convention and would undoubtedly approve of the President's nominee.

On the resignation of Spiro T. Agnew in 1973, President Nixon submitted the name of Gerald R. Ford to the Congress. After some legislative infighting, the Senate assigned the task of holding hearings to its Committee on Rules and Administration, and the House delegated the responsibility to its Judiciary Committee. After public hearings and intensive investigation, each committee reported its findings and recommendations to its chamber, which then voted separately on the President's nominee, confirming him.

A similar procedure was followed when President Ford nominated Nelson A. Rockefeller and the Congress elected him as Vice-President on December 19, 1974. For the first time in our history, the United States had both a President and Vice-President who had not been elected by the people. However, had the Twenty-Fifth Amendment not been in effect, the office of President, upon Agnew and Nixon's resignations, would have devolved upon the Speaker of the House, a member of the opposite political party from that which had won the 1972 presidential election. Moreover, the office of Vice President would have been vacant from October, 1973 until January, 1977. The Twenty-Fifth Amendment worked exceedingly well in this crucial period of our history.

Section 3   President Designates Vice-President as Acting President

WHENEVER THE PRESIDENT TRANSMITS TO THE PRESIDENT PRO TEMPORE OF THE SENATE AND THE SPEAKER OF THE HOUSE OF REPRESENTATIVES HIS WRITTEN DECLARATION THAT HE IS UNABLE TO DISCHARGE THE POWERS AND DUTIES OF HIS OFFICE, AND UNTIL HE TRANSMITS TO THEM A WRITTEN DECLARATION TO THE CONTRARY, SUCH POWERS AND DUTIES SHALL BE DISCHARGED BY THE VICE-PRESIDENT AS ACTING PRESIDENT.

Several times in our history, presidents have been so disabled that they could not carry on the duties of the office. Presidents Abraham Lincoln and James A. Garfield lingered at death's door for hours and days after being felled by assassins' bullets. Presidents Wilson, Franklin Roosevelt, Eisenhower, and Lyndon Johnson suffered major illnesses while in office. No explicit constitutional procedure existed to permit the Vice-President to exercise any presidential power during these grave emergencies. In recent years,

Presidents Eisenhower, Kennedy, and Johnson entered into private agreements with their respective Vice-Presidents spelling out the circumstances when the Vice-President would serve as acting President because of presidential disability. Though helpful, these private arrangements lacked constitutional sanction and placed the Vice-President in a most difficult position. This section clarifies the procedure.

First, the President, in writing, notifies the Speaker of the House and the President pro tempore of the Senate that he is unable to discharge the duties of the office. Thereupon, the Vice-President *acts* as President with all powers and duties of that office until such time as the President notifies, again in writing, the two congressional leaders that he is able to resume all the powers and duties of the presidency. President Ronald Reagan, in July, 1985, notified the Speaker and president-pro-tem of the Senate both before and after a serious surgical operation, even though he had doubts about the efficacy of Section 3.

This section takes care of the case of presidential disability where the President recognizes his situation and therefore initiates the action. It likewise provides for the obvious recovery of the President and the recognition of this fact by both the Vice-President and the Congress. The following section attempts to deal with the stickier situations where the President either cannot, or will not, initiate the temporary transfer of power to the Vice-President.

Section 4   Vice-President and Cabinet Declare Presidential Disability

WHENEVER THE VICE-PRESIDENT AND A MAJORITY OF EITHER THE PRINCIPAL OFFICERS OF THE EXECUTIVE DEPARTMENTS OR OF SUCH OTHER BODY AS CONGRESS MAY BY LAW PROVIDE, TRANSMIT TO THE PRESIDENT PRO TEMPORE OF THE SENATE AND THE SPEAKER OF THE HOUSE OF REPRESENTATIVES THEIR WRITTEN DECLARATION THAT THE PRESIDENT IS UNABLE TO DISCHARGE THE POWERS AND DUTIES OF HIS OFFICE, THE VICE-PRESIDENT SHALL IMMEDIATELY

ASSUME THE POWERS AND DUTIES OF THE OFFICE AS ACTING
PRESIDENT.

Note that this section relieves the Vice-President of the sole responsibility for determining the President's disability. The procedure requires the Vice-President to consult with the heads of the major executive departments (the cabinet). If a majority of the cabinet and the Vice-President agree, they must send to the Speaker of the House and the President pro tempore of the Senate a written declaration stating that the President is unable to carry on the duties of the office. Once this declaration is sent to Congress, the Vice-President immediately becomes *acting* President. Note that at this stage the Congress makes no determination of whether or not the President is truly disabled. Congress is required to accept the decision submitted by the Vice-President and the cabinet. However, in the remaining portion of Section 4, the Congress may get involved.

Section 4 [*continued*] Congress Decides Disability

THEREAFTER, WHEN THE PRESIDENT TRANSMITS TO THE
PRESIDENT PRO TEMPORE OF THE SENATE AND THE SPEAKER OF
THE HOUSE OF REPRESENTATIVES HIS WRITTEN DECLARATION THAT
NO INABILITY EXISTS, HE SHALL RESUME THE POWERS AND DUTIES
OF HIS OFFICE UNLESS THE VICE-PRESIDENT AND A MAJORITY OF
EITHER THE PRINCIPAL OFFICERS OF THE EXECUTIVE DEPARTMENT
OR OF SUCH OTHER BODY AS CONGRESS MAY BY LAW PROVIDE,
TRANSMIT WITHIN FOUR DAYS TO THE PRESIDENT PRO TEMPORE
OF THE SENATE AND THE SPEAKER OF THE HOUSE OF
REPRESENTATIVES THEIR WRITTEN DECLARATION THAT THE
PRESIDENT IS UNABLE TO DISCHARGE THE POWERS AND DUTIES OF
HIS OFFICE. THEREUPON CONGRESS SHALL DECIDE THE ISSUE,
ASSEMBLING WITHIN FORTY-EIGHT HOURS FOR THAT PURPOSE IF
NOT IN SESSION. IF THE CONGRESS, WITHIN TWENTY-ONE DAYS
AFTER RECEIPT OF THE LATTER WRITTEN DECLARATION, OR, IF
CONGRESS IS NOT IN SESSION, WITHIN TWENTY-ONE DAYS AFTER·
CONGRESS IS REQUIRED TO ASSEMBLE, DETERMINES BY TWO-

THIRDS VOTE OF BOTH HOUSES THAT THE PRESIDENT IS UNABLE TO DISCHARGE THE POWERS AND DUTIES OF HIS OFFICE, THE VICE-PRESIDENT SHALL CONTINUE TO DISCHARGE THE SAME AS ACTING PRESIDENT; OTHERWISE, THE PRESIDENT SHALL RESUME THE POWERS AND DUTIES OF HIS OFFICE.

Even though the Vice-President and cabinet have certified that the President is disabled, the President, by this clause, may reclaim his powers by notifying the Speaker and the President pro tempore that *no* inability exists. The President's written declaration is conclusive evidence of his fitness to exercise the powers of the office *unless* the Vice-President and a majority of the cabinet *again* submit a written declaration, within four days of the President's letter, stating that the President is unable to discharge the duties of the office. Thus there would be a conflict between the President, who says he is fit, and the Vice-President and cabinet, who say he is not. This is when Congress has to step in and decide the issue.

The Congress is required to assemble within forty-eight hours after receiving the Vice-President's and cabinet's declaration. It is given twenty-one days to settle the question of presidential disability. Because of the serious nature of the question, an extraordinary vote is required, and the burden of proof is placed on the Vice-President. Thus a two-thirds vote is necessary in each house to uphold the vice-presidential claim that the President is unable to discharge the duties of the office. If both houses vote the two-thirds majority, then the Vice-President continues as acting President. If a two-thirds vote is not obtained in either house, then the President immediately resumes the powers and duties of the office. It also appears that if Congress fails to resolve the issue by the end of the twenty-one day period, the President resumes his office.

Left to speculation, at this time, is the question of the President's options in the event Congress does uphold the vice-presidential claim as acting President. That is, how often could the President initiate congressional determination after having been rejected? We can hope that Section 4 will never have to be used.

Amendment 26

Proposed March 23, 1971   Ratified June 30, 1971

Eighteen-Year-Old Vote

Several states had permitted eighteen-, nineteen-, and twenty-year-olds to vote in all elections, while other states had rejected proposals to lower the voting age. In 1970, Congress passed the Voting Rights Act which, among other provisions, lowered the minimum voting age for all elections to eighteen. The act was challenged in the courts, and the Supreme Court ruled that Congress had the power to set standards for federal elections but could not do so for state and local elections. The effect of this decision was to create confusion and turmoil among state election officials, especially when federal and state elections were held at the same time. The Twenty-Sixth Amendment was introduced to clarify and systematize the process. The quick ratification reflected not only the desire to stabilize the voting age, but also reflected the popular attitude that if eighteen-year-olds can be drafted to fight a war, then they should be permitted to have a voice in selecting their governmental leaders.

Section 1   Eighteen-Year-Old Suffrage

THE RIGHT OF CITIZENS OF THE UNITED STATES, WHO ARE EIGHTEEN YEARS OF AGE OR OLDER, TO VOTE SHALL NOT BE DENIED OR ABRIDGED BY THE UNITED STATES OR BY ANY STATE ON ACCOUNT OF AGE.

Section 2   Enforcement

THE CONGRESS SHALL HAVE THE POWER TO ENFORCE THIS ARTICLE BY APPROPRIATE LEGISLATION.

Note that this amendment is phrased in the same way as the Fifteenth and Nineteenth Amendments. It is negative in character. It means that the states, and the United States, cannot use age, specifically an age of eighteen or older, as a basis of denying the privilege of voting. It does not mean that all eighteen-year-olds are automatically enfranchised. They, like other potential voters, must meet the other qualifications that states impose on their citizens.

Amendment 27

Proposed September 25, 1789   Ratified May 12, 1992

Congressional Compensation

NO LAW VARYING THE COMPENSATION FOR THE SERVICES OF THE SENATORS AND REPRESENTATIVES SHALL TAKE EFFECT UNTIL AN ELECTION OF REPRESENTATIVES SHALL HAVE INTERVENED.

This amendment was proposed by James Madison in 1789 as part of a package of twelve additions to the original Constitution. Only six states had ratified this proposal by the time, December 15, 1791, ten other amendments had received the requisite number of ratification; thus it never became a part of the famous Bill of Rights. One state ratified it in 1873, but another century passed before other states began to approve it during the 1970s and 1980s.

Though the necessary three-fourths states had ratified the proposal by May 12, 1992, serious doubts were raised as to the validity of the process since the ratification had extended over a period of 203 years. General opinion tended to treat the amendment as "constitutionally dead," since it had not been ratified within a reasonable time from its submittal to the states. Congressional uncertainty over the amendment's applicability was manifest by the scheduling of committee hearings to take expert testimony. However, on May 13, 1992, the Archivist of the United States announced he would certify the adoption of the Twenty-Seventh Amendment, thus forcing congressional opponents to back away from any immediate constitutional challenge, though a later one could ensue since 1993 was a year in which automatic cost of living adjustments (COLAS) was scheduled for congress.

Proposed Amendment

Proposed March 22, 1972

Equal Rights

As of June 30, 1982, only thirty-five states had ratified this amendment.

Even after the adoption of the Nineteenth Amendment, which banned sexual discrimination in the voting privilege, there were a number of prominent women, as well women's groups, who felt that the amendment did not go far enough. Considerable discrimination existed in such areas as employment opportunities, legal standing, marriage and divorce, property-owning, etc.; and this stimulated a concerted effort to secure the passage of this amendment.

In 1971 the Supreme Court had ruled that the equal-protection-of-the-laws clause prohibited unreasonable discrimination based purely on sex. Leaders of the Women's Liberation movement, however, pushed for a constitutional amendment as providing more permanent protection than a court decision, which could possibly be modified in future cases.

In the resolution forwarding this Amendment to the states (but not in the Amendment itself), Congress set a seven-year time limit for ratification (March 22, 1979). When the dead-line approached and the requisite number of approvals had not been obtained, Congress, again by resolution, extended the deadline to June 30, 1982. In December, 1981, a District Court judge ruled Congress could not extend the deadline; however, the Supreme Court stayed the execution of this ruling until it had the opportunity to hear the arguments and to deliberate on a decision. Later, when the extended deadline had passed and the amendment still lacked three states for ratification, the constitutional questions of time extension and rescinding a prior ratification became moot.

Section 1   Equality of Rights

EQUALITY OF RIGHTS UNDER THE LAW SHALL NOT BE DENIED

OR ABRIDGED BY THE UNITED STATES OR BY ANY STATE ON
ACCOUNT OF SEX.

Note again that this amendment is phrased in the negative, similar
to the Fifteenth and Nineteenth Amendments. It simply means that a
person's sex, whether female or male, shall not be used as the sole
basis of denying equal rights. The amendment applies equally to the
protection of male rights. The intent of the amendment is to outlaw
not only government laws and regulations, but also private rules and
policies that foster discrimination. For example, some states prohibit
women from serving on juries. This amendment would make such a
practice unconstitutional.

Section 2   Enforcement

THE CONGRESS SHALL HAVE POWER TO ENFORCE, BY
APPROPRIATE LEGISLATION, THE PROVISIONS OF THIS ARTICLE.

Even without the authority of this section, Congress has passed
laws prohibiting various types of discrimination in both governmental
and private sectors of our society. A question that is being raised
during some ratification debates is whether or not this amendment
would prohibit governments from passing laws that are favorable
only to women. For example, most states have various health and
safety laws that require special privileges for female workers, e.g.,
work breaks and pregnancy leaves. Another question debated is
whether women could be drafted into the armed services.

Section 3   Effective Date

THIS AMENDMENT SHALL TAKE EFFECT TWO YEARS AFTER
DATE OF RATIFICATION.

The reason for this section is to give the states, local governments,
agencies, etc., sufficient time to make their rules and regulations
conform to this amendment.

Proposed Amendment

Proposed August 22, 1978

Representation for the District of Columbia

As of December 1, 1981, ten states had ratified this amendment. From its inception, the District of Columbia has been subject to the control of Congress in accordance with Article I, Section 8, Clause 17. Throughout its history, the structure of government of the District took many forms but basically the permanent residents had no voice or vote in the selection of officials who governed them or in the election of federal officers. In 1961, the Twenty-Third Amendment was approved which entitled District residents to vote for presidential electors. In 1971, Congress allowed the people to elect a non-voting delegate to the House of Representatives. In 1975, Congress passed and the people approved a Home Rule charter whereby the residents could elect their own Mayor and City Council. Finally, in 1978, Congress, in a move to grant political equality to the approximate 700,000 residents of the District of Columbia, submitted the following amendment to the states for ratification. If approved by the required thirty-eight states, this proposed amendment would repeal the Twenty-Third Amendment and would treat the District of Columbia "as though it were a state" for purposes of representation in Congress, presidential elections, and ratifying constitutional amendments.

Section 1   District Treated as a State

FOR PURPOSE OF REPRESENTATION IN THE CONGRESS, ELECTION OF THE PRESIDENT AND VICE PRESIDENT, AND ARTICLE V OF THIS CONSTITUTION, THE DISTRICT CONSTITUTING THE SEAT GOVERNMENT OF THE UNITED STATES SHALL BE TREATED AS THOUGH IT WERE A STATE.

Section 2   Limiting Application to District

THE EXERCISE OF THE RIGHTS AND POWERS CONFERRED

UNDER THIS ARTICLE SHALL BE BY THE PEOPLE OF THE DISTRICT CONSTITUTING THE SEAT OF GOVERNMENT, AND AS SHALL BE PROVIDED BY THE CONGRESS.

Section 3　　Repeal Twenty-Third Amendment

THE TWENTY-THIRD ARTICLE OF AMENDMENT TO THE CONSTITUTION OF THE UNITED STATES IS HEREBY REPEALED.

Section 4　　Time Limit

THIS ARTICLE SHALL BE INOPERATIVE, UNLESS IT SHALL HAVE BEEN RATIFIED AS AN AMENDMENT TO THE CONSTITUTION BY THE LEGISLATURES OF THREE-FOURTHS OF THE SEVERAL STATES WITHIN SEVEN YEARS FROM THE DATE OF ITS SUBMISSION.

Chapter 6

Relations Between the Nation and the States

The United States of America is a federal state. This means that the powers that "We the people" permit all governments to exercise are divided between our national government and our state governments. Furthermore, "We the people" have retained certain other powers. The Constitution of the United States is the instrument that makes this division of power. The Constitution receives its authority from the people of the United States. In addition, each of the fifty states has its own constitution deriving authority from the people of the state. Therefore, Americans live under two constitutions; both spring from the will of the people, and both act directly upon the people. This is essential to a federal system.

At first glance, such a system appears complicated; actually it is not. The United States Constitution provides the grand divisions of power between the national government and the states. The state constitutions apportion the powers that have been reserved to them among the various branches and municipalities within the state governments. This chapter outlines the distribution of powers and the constitutional relationships between the two levels of government.

Distribution of Powers

<u>Residual Powers.</u> The national government is often called a government of enumerated or delegated powers. It may exercise only those powers that have been given to it, either directly or by

implication, by the Constitution. Some of these powers can be exercised only by the national government, while others may be shared with the states.

The states, on the other hand, are often referred to as governments of *residual powers*. They possessed certain powers before the Constitution was formulated and they retained a great many of these powers after its adoption. There is no enumeration of the powers that the states possess, not even in the United States Constitution. The powers exercised by the states are discovered through a process of elimination. If we eliminate those powers delegated to the national government and those that are forbidden to the states, the powers that then remain (the residue) may be recognized as belonging to the states.

The addition of state powers to those exercised by the national government would not give a complete and grand total of governmental authority. Recollect that our governments are *limited governments*. Certain rights have been retained by the people, even though there is no exact listing or description of these rights (Amendment 9). Furthermore, the national government has been forbidden to do certain things (Article I, Section 9) that state governments are likewise prohibited from doing (Article I, Section 10), and both governments are banned from exercising still other powers. An understanding of these general principles makes it easier to set down the distribution of powers between the national and state governments. The following six categories, though not all-inclusive, include the most important powers:

(1) Powers exercised *exclusively* by the national government:
   1. Regulating interstate and foreign commerce.
   2. Conducting international relations.
   3. Preparing amendments to the Constitution.
   4. Settling disputes between states.
   5. Settling disputes involving foreign diplomats, admiralty cases, and cases where the United States is a party.
   6. Admitting new states to the Union.

(2) Powers exercised *exclusively* by the state governments:
   1. Creating local units of government, such as counties, cities, and villages.
   2. Providing rules to govern the conduct of individual toward individual.
   3. Ratifying constitutional amendments.

(3) Powers exercised *concurrently* by the national and state governments:
   1. Levying taxes and borrowing money.
   2. Naturalizing citizens.
   3. Settling disputes involving citizens of different states.

(4) Powers *prohibited* to the national government:
   1. Depriving persons of their freedom and protections under the Bill of Rights.
   2. Suspending the writ of habeas corpus arbitrarily.
   3. Levying a direct tax, without reference to population.

(5) Powers *prohibited* to the state governments:
   1. Making treaties or entering into alliances.
   2. Levying tonnage, import, or export taxes arbitrarily.
   3. Coining money or impairing the obligations of contracts.
   4. Depriving persons of their privileges and immunities of U.S. citizenship or equal protection of the laws.

(6) Powers *prohibited* to both the national and state governments:
   1. Depriving persons of life, liberty, and property without due process of law.
   2. Taking private property without just compensation.
   3. Depriving persons of the right to vote, because of color, race, or sex.
   4. Passing *ex post facto* laws or bills of attainder.
   5. Granting titles of nobility.

Reciprocal Duties

Our constitutional system is not a one-way street. Though the national constitution and national laws are supreme and state laws cannot conflict, there are duties and obligations that the national government owes to the states. Likewise, the states have their duties toward the national government and toward one another. Briefly, these reciprocal duties are as follows:

Obligations of the Nation to the States.

1. Protection against foreign and domestic violence

Any invasion of a state would, of course, be an invasion of the United States. The national government must go to the aid of the stricken state as quickly and powerfully as possible. The state, naturally, would meet such an attack with all the force at its command.

The national government is also duty-bound to keep the peace and order of the nation. Normally the states carry out this function and do it exceedingly well. However, if asked to interfere, or if federal law and property are involved, the national government can step in with its forces, even over the objections of state authorities.

2. Respect for territorial integrity and identity

No state may be divided up without the consent of its legislature, nor may a state be expelled from the Union. Furthermore, the Civil War demonstrated that a state may not withdraw from the Union. Congress has power to admit new states, but no territory may force Congress to admit it. Once admitted, a new state is equal, politically and legally, to all the other states.

3. Guarantee of a republican form of government

While neither the Constitution nor court decisions define precisely a "republican form of government," a general understanding has emerged. Basically, it means a representative form of government as distinguished from a monarchy, oligarchy, or dictatorship. Within the general meaning of this guarantee, the states have a large degree of control over their internal governmental arrangements. They would have to go far afield in order to evoke the discipline of the national government. A revolutionary government would not be tolerated. If two governments existed, each claiming to be the lawful one, the national government would probably have to make the final decision between them. Thus, behind their own state officials, the people of a state have the power of the national government to enforce a representative form of government.

4. Representation in Congress

Each state is guaranteed equality of representation in the Senate. In addition, each state is entitled to at least one Representative in the House. Through these constitutional conditions, the separate entities of the states are recognized and are protected by representatives of their own choosing.

It is difficult to imagine how a state could lose representation in Congress. In 1954, a Senate resolution that would have declared the 1952 senatorial election in New Mexico void and prohibited the governor from filling the vacancy, was soundly defeated. Many of the Senators believed that this resolution violated the constitutional guarantee of equality of representation.

Obligations of States to the Nation.

1. Participation in the electoral process of government

This is a very important function. The national government relies upon the states to establish qualifications for voters and manage the election processes. If a state refuses to participate, or provides inadequate facilities, it not only acts against that state's prestige, but also weakens the structure and spirit of the federal system.

2. Participation in the amendment process

States are essential to the amendment process. It is not necessary that they approve every amendment submitted to them. But it is in the best interest and protection of its citizens that a state consider and discuss the merits of a proposed amendment. Then, by positive action, it may either approve or disapprove the proposal.

3. Maintenance of law and order

The first and primary responsibility for the maintenance of law and order rests with the states. They cannot shirk this duty. Public violence in one state affects not only the state concerned, but neighboring states as well. Although the federal government stands ready to lend assistance, the states are not hasty in requesting national interference. Nevertheless, the federal government will exercise its powers even over the objections of the states.

4. Maintenance of a republican form of government

This again is a primary function of a state. Appeals to the national government are not frequent. The duty of maintaining a republican form of government does not place a state in a political straitjacket, since states have freedom to experiment with their internal governmental structures. A one-house or unicameral legislature is as representative as a bicameral system. Giving the people a direct voice in deciding questions of policy also is within a republican form of government. The whole nation has a stake in the prosperity and stability of one state; that state has an obligation to fulfill this expectation.

Obligations of States to States

1. Recognizing the legal acts and processes of other states

The famous "full faith and credit" clause requires a state to honor and respect the public records, acts, and judicial proceedings of another state. Records pertaining to deeds, wills, marriages, divorces, and contracts are very important in our society. Together with judgments handed down by the courts, they are not to be treated lightly. Such matters come within the powers of the states, and common sense tells us that they should be uniformly protected throughout the entire United States. Otherwise, it might be possible for a person to move into another state and thereby evade his or her legal responsibilities or debts. Imagine the trouble that would result if state courts refused to honor business contracts signed in other states. It makes for easier living when we know that other states will honor our valid records and documents.

2. Returning fugitives from justice

In this age of rapid transportation, it is relatively easy for a criminal to flee his or her state and hide elsewhere. Unless there were some way to return these criminals to the state in which the crime was committed, many would escape their deserved punishment. The interstate rendition provision in the Constitution places an obligation upon a state to return wanted persons. The state that captures the fugitive can neither punish the criminal nor enforce the criminal law of the other state. However, it can do the next best thing by returning him or her to the state where he or she committed the crime. In this manner, all the states benefit by the removal of a menace to society.

3. Recognizing the rights of interstate citizenship

Consider the advantages enjoyed by Americans in comparison with citizens of European countries. We may travel 3,000 miles or more without being stopped by customs posts or blockades or an "iron curtain." We may come and go as we please throughout the fifty states. The interstate citizenship provision helps to break down artificial barriers of trade, communication, and travel. It has helped to weld the states together into one united union. It places an obligation on a state to treat citizens of other states fairly—or as fairly as it treats its own citizens. States must recognize that other citizens have the right to buy, manage, or sell property without discrimination. Of course, it may reserve political privileges for its own citizens, but the enjoyment of everyday, ordinary rights is the common property of all the citizens of all states. How valuable this freedom of personal and commercial exchange has become is evidenced by the political and social agonies many European countries experienced as they implemented the European Economic Community which will allow citizens and goods to move freely around European nations as their counterparts do in the United States.

4. Settling disputes peaceably

No matter how angry the people of one state may be with those of another state, there is no violence. Disputes between states are settled in a peaceful manner, usually by the courts. In a few instances such disputes are settled by interstate compacts or agreements.

5. Maintenance of cooperation

The key to the successful working of our federal system lies in the friendly cooperation existing among all members of the Union. Prohibitions and compulsions are at a minimum. The states quickly learned that mutual help benefits everyone. Today there are scores of examples of this cooperative spirit—extending from formalized agreements over the distribution of water to tacit understandings of aid and comfort in times of crisis or disaster. It is an old cliche that "a chain is as strong as its weakest link." By joining together in a spirit of cooperation, the states are able to maintain and extend their strength and power.

Federalism at Work

Ours is a dynamic federalism. As time passes and conditions change, so, too, do our governmental responsibilities. Each level of government has been entrusted with important and ample powers. It is the responsibility of those whom we elect to public office to use these powers wisely and effectively. In the course of 205 years our nation has been transformed from a rural-agricultural society into a predominantly urban-industrial community. It is logical to assume that our governmental machinery has tried to keep pace with this tremendous development. Functions and services that were either nonexistent or carried on by private individuals a century ago are now expected and accepted duties of government. A century ago every able-bodied male was required to work several days every year on the public highways. Such a system of highway construction and repair today would prove quite inefficient and inadequate. Thus, the automobile is just one of many mechanical and scientific inventions that has created new demands on our governments.

Federal Expansion. As our nation developed physically, nationally, and politically, more and more powers were exercised by the national government. Washington began to enter areas and do things traditionally performed by state governments or not done at all. This growth of influence on the part of the national government was not a planned affair but, like Topsy, it "just growed."

The source of some of this centralization may be traced directly to constitutional amendments. The Thirteenth, Fourteenth, Fifteenth, Sixteenth, and Nineteenth Amendments have either limited the powers of the states or else conferred new powers on the national government. Also, the extraordinary growth of our networks of transportation, commerce and communications brought forth regulations by the national government. The nationwide activities of these enterprises were of such great importance that the national government appeared to be the logical government to deal with them. Still other national powers evolved by way of implication from expressed or delegated powers.

The financial resources of the federal government also contributed to the increase of authority in Washington. The national government was, and still is, able to tax more and greater sources of revenue than any single state. By dangling gifts of money, called grants-in-aid, in front of the financially embarrassed states, the federal government is able to secure their cooperation in a number of joint programs. Grants-in-aid for highway building and maintenance, agricultural research and welfare services are just a few of these mutual programs. Moreover, some state officials have been employed by the federal government to help administer and supervise federal programs.

A number of changes have come about as a result of direct appeals by the states for aid in enforcing state laws. Thus federal officers help in capturing kidnappers, recovering stolen automobiles, breaking up narcotic rings, or eliminating white slavery. Congress passed laws restricting the effects of gambling, an area always considered within the police power of the states. Similarly, the federal government performs a number of research or experimental services for the states as well as cooperating in such voluntary programs as police training by the FBI or fingerprint service.

Effect of Emergencies. Needless to say the depression of the 1930's, World War II, the Korean and Vietnam controversies, and world oil politics have had a great effect on relations between the nation and the states. Each national crisis has tended to leave the federal government with a little more power than it had at the outset. Once any government starts to operate in an area it is very difficult to remove it. During the depression the federal government appropriated large sums of money for direct aid to states and cities. A number of special agencies were created to deal with the unemployment situation. Some of these agencies continued to operate long after they outlived their usefulness.

World War II came, and new industries sprang up all over the country, many in small cities and towns. Thousands of workers flocked to new jobs. Hundreds of military posts were established, often in sparsely settled areas. The local units of government were unable to provide the needed facilities, even if they had the necessary money. The states likewise could not finance new water, gas, light, sewage, or housing facilities. Again, the federal government had to enter the picture to deal with problems caused by our involvement in Asian conflicts and the Arab oil politics of the 1960s and 1970s. It is an old saying that "he who pays the piper can call the tune." Control over money almost always means the power to decide where the money shall be spent, by whom and for what purposes. The federal government was "calling the tune" in these cases.

Future of the States. But the concentration of authority in the national government does not mean that the states are, or should be, relegated to an inferior or unimportant position. They are essential to a federal form of government. Let us not forget that the states also have expanded their activities in the past century. A quick check of the budget figures covering this period will readily confirm this statement. The people expect, and the states are giving them, many more services. The same situation is true of local governments.

The states are mighty important to our everyday living; so much so that we take many things for granted. The most significant relationships of our family, social, and economic lives are dependent upon state laws—marriage, contracts, charters, crimes, our person-to-person conduct, our voting rights, and our local units of government obtain their force from the state. We can experiment with political devices and ideas. Those devices that prove successful (such as the initiative, the referendum, and city manager) may be adopted by other states. The unsuccessful experiments, in turn, have not endangered the nation.

Ours is a dynamic federalism, changing emphasis as the nation has expanded and matured over a continent during two centuries. The relationships between the states and the federal government have inevitably changed with these geographic, economic, and political factors, as well as with the expectations, demands, and limitations imposed by the successive generations of citizens on their governments. During these two centuries our federalism has evolved through a series of stages variously labeled by scholars as constitutional federalism, dual federalism, cooperative federalism, permissive federalism, and what in the 1980s is sometimes referred to as fiscal federalism.

With the coming to power of the administration of President Ronald W. Reagan and a more conservative Congress, a "New Federalism" was initiated. The Reagan federalism, continued during the term of President George W. Bush, had as its two main themes a reduction in federal expenditures and a return to state control and financing of a number of heretofore federal programs. The buildup of a huge deficit over these twelve years, sparked by a movement for "change" resulted in President Bill Clinton's election in 1992 and a probable new redefinition of federalism.

The future of the states in our federal system is promising. States have discovered that mutual cooperation and formalized agreements have been successful in slowing down the trend toward federal centralization. The states have also learned that there is no substitute for thoughtful, needed legislation and wise and efficient administration. An alert and interested public, recognizing that there are many problems to be solved, can best help the cause of good American government by giving active and intelligent advice and support to their chosen public officials.

Index